Body Talk

D0850866

Body Talk

Teaching Students with Disabilities about Body Language

Pat Crissey

Woodbine House ■ 2013

© 2013 Pat Crissey

All rights reserved.

Published in the United States of America by Woodbine House, Inc., 6510 Bells Mill Road, Bethesda, MD. 800-843-7323. www.woodbinehouse.com

Illustrations on pages 90 and 91 are from Ann M. Martin—THE BABY-SITTERS CLUB: CHRISTY'S GREAT IDEA: A Graphic Novel by Raina Telgemeier, Scholastic Inc./Graphix. Text copyright © 2006 by Ann M. Martin, art copyright © 2006 by Raina Telgemeier. Reprinted by permission.

Library of Congress Cataloging in Publication Data

Crissey, Pat, 1946-
  Body talk : teaching students with disabilities about body language / by Pat Crissey. -- First edition.
       page cm
  Includes index.
  ISBN 978-1-60613-175-6
  1. Nonverbal communication in children. 2. Body language--Study and teaching. 3. Children with disabilities--Education. I. Title.
  BF723.C57C75 2013
  153.6'9071--dc23
                                                                                            2012049094

First Edition
10 9 8 7 6 5 4 3 2 1

To my son, Noah, and daughter-in-law, Soraya,
for their help with the artwork.

And to my husband, Rob, for his continual loving support.

Table of Contents

Introduction

The ability to understand and use appropriate nonverbal communication is essential to successful social interactions*. If we don't understand what others are truly communicating, how can we respond appropriately?

While there has been a growing awareness of the importance of body language and the challenges it presents to some individuals, including many on the autism spectrum, parents, teachers, and therapists often remain at a loss about how to best help children in this area. How does one go about teaching something so complex, yet so intuitive? *Body Talk: Teaching Students with Disabilities about Body Language* breaks this incredibly complex topic into teachable components.

Body Talk was written to continue where my earlier book *Getting the Message: Learning to Read Facial Expressions* left off. For that reason, basic information about how to teach facial expressions is provided, along with ideas for activities, but step-by-step instruction and detailed activities are not provided.

The focus of *Body Talk* is on the other types of body language: posture, orientation, eye gaze, personal space, touching, and gestures. In addition, a large part of the curriculum focuses on reading body language *in context*. The final unit, "Putting It All Together," uses a wide variety of activities to encourage students to interpret all types of body language, including facial expressions, within everyday situations.

---

* Cynthia Burggraf Torppa, "Nonverbal Communication: Teaching Your Child the Skills of Social Success," *Family and Consumer Sciences Fact Sheet* (Columbus, OH: The Ohio State University Extension, 2009), 1.

Chapter 1

Understanding Emotions

Children need a basic understanding of emotions before learning about body language. The ability to equate different postures, gestures, and facial expressions with certain emotions has no practical value if the child does not understand what it means to feel those emotions. Therefore, the first step in teaching body language is to determine the student's understanding of emotions.

The following activities can be used to assess the child's understanding, as well as to provide opportunities to explore the meaning of different emotions. While a basic understanding of emotions is a prerequisite for learning about body language, it is not necessary to delay teaching body language until the student has a thorough understanding of a wide array of emotions. You will be continuing to teach about emotions as you teach body language. Once the student recognizes basic emotions in himself, he is probably ready to move ahead.

Which Emotions to Teach?

Deciding which emotions to cover can be difficult since there is a virtually endless list from which to choose. The main consideration is which emotions are most important for the child to understand, and this differs, of course, with age and level of functioning.

Experts differ somewhat as to which emotions they label as primary emotions. These primary or universal emotions are unique, different from other emotions, and have associated facial expressions that are recognized throughout the world. Six emotions that are commonly considered primary emotions are: *happiness, sadness, anger, fear, surprise,* and *disgust*. When teaching emotions, it's best to begin with these.

Of course there are many other emotions, often called secondary emotions. These may be a combination of more than one primary emotion. For example, remorse is often seen as a combination of sadness and disgust.

There are other emotions that are subsets of the basic emotions, but with a more narrow description. For example, feeling worried or terrified are both types of fear, but at different levels of intensity. Or a particular emotion may provide an explanation as to the cause of another emotion. A lonely person feels sad because he is alone. When someone is proud, he feels happy because of what he has accomplished.

The following is a suggested list of emotions to teach. Begin with the basic six and add other emotions as students are ready.

1. Happy—pleased, glad, content, excited, ecstatic
2. Sad—unhappy, hurt, discouraged
3. Angry—mad, upset, frustrated, furious, resentful, impatient, furious
4. Scared—afraid, worried, nervous, concerned, frightened, alarmed, anxious, fearful
5. Surprised—shocked, astonished, amazed
6. Disgusted—to make one sick, repelled, revolted

Other common emotions:

- interested, enthusiastic
- bored
- contemptuous
- grateful
- confused
- jealous, envious
- embarrassed
- ashamed, sorry
- shy
- proud
- grouchy, grumpy, irritable

Introducing Emotions

How Does It Make You Feel?

For students who have little understanding of emotions, begin by collecting pictures of items or situations that elicit different feelings, such as cute kittens and ice cream for happy feelings, and a broken toy or people waving good-bye for sadness. Start with a couple of the basic emotions, and add other emotions as the child is ready. Write the emotion words on top of large sheets of paper and have students place pictures on the appropriate sheet of paper. (See the example below.)

What makes me feel scared

What makes me feel happy

For students who have difficulty reading, use pictures or simple line drawings of faces depicting the different emotions. More advanced students could make written lists of items and situations that elicit different emotions.

What Does It Feel Like?

Have students describe what it feels like when they are feeling happy, sad, angry, scared, surprised, and disgusted. If students are able to read, write their responses on chart paper. See examples below.

Happy:
- I like how my body feels
- I like people
- I have lots of energy
- I feel like smiling and laughing

Sad:
- I feel all alone
- I don't have much energy, don't feel like doing things
- Nothing seems interesting or fun
- I don't feel like smiling or laughing; I feel like crying

Angry:
- It seems like everyone is mean
- My body feels tight
- I feel like I'm going to explode
- I want to hit or kick
- I want to yell or scream

Scared:
- I want to hide
- My hands get sweaty
- My stomach hurts
- My body feels tight
- My heart beats really fast

Surprised:
- I feel really awake
- I breathe in really fast
- My heart beats fast
- At first I feel scared, then I know there's nothing scary

Disgusted:
- I want to back away, or turn away
- It makes me feel sick to my stomach
- Makes me wrinkle my nose, like something really stinks

Some students may have difficulty picturing and describing emotions they are not currently feeling. Try to catch the students when they are feeling different emotions, and ask how they are feeling at the moment and help them label their emotional state.

Teaching Activities

Feelings Check In

Schedule a few minutes each day to have students tell how they are feeling, and, if students are able, have them tell why they are feeling that way. It is also good to take time to do this after an event that arouses strong feelings. If needed, use a chart with visuals, as shown.

Sorting Emotions

Place pictures illustrating emotions or emotion words on individual cards, one emotion per card. You can use either pictures of different facial expressions or situations associated with different emotions, such as riding on a carousel or experiencing a lightning storm. Have students sort the cards, putting similar cards together. How you ask students to categorize the cards should depend on their abilities. For example, they could be sorted into emotions you like to feel and those you don't like, or things that make you feel sad versus afraid, etc. More advanced students could sort emotion words into groups that are similar, such as worried, scared, terrified, etc.

Feeling Books

Have students collect pictures from magazines showing things that make them feel happy, sad, angry, scared, surprised, and disgusted. Use the pictures to create books entitled "What Makes Me Feel Happy." Students could also create happy books about themselves using photos you take of them doing things they like.

Repeat the above activity, creating books that illustrate different emotions and different intensities of the primary emotions.

Read about Emotions

An excellent way to help students understand emotions is to read and discuss storybooks or books describing feelings. Books with illustrations or photos are the most helpful for understanding the connection between feelings and body language. Below are some suggestions. Primary level books are generally considered appropriate for kindergarten through second grade, and intermediate level for third grade and above.

Books Describing a Variety of Emotions:

- Avery, C. (1992). *Everybody Has Feelings: Todos Tenemos Sentimientos*. Open Hand Publishing. (primary, bilingual)
- Berendes, M. (2008). *Feelings: Las Emociones*. The Child's World. (primary, bilingual)
- Feeney, K. (2002). *Feel Good: Understand Your Emotions*. Bridgesport Books. (primary)
- Kalman, B. (2010). *I Have Feelings/Tengo Sentimientos (My World/Mi Mundo)*. Crabtree Publishing Co. (primary, bilingual)
- Lamia, M. *Understanding Myself: A Kid's Guide to Intense Emotions and Strong Feelings*. Magination Press. (intermediate)
- Leeper, A. (2005). *Tengo Sentimientos (Tu y Yo)*. Heinemann-Raintree. (primary, Spanish)
- Madison, L. (2002). *The Feelings Book: The Care and Keeping of Your Emotions (American Girl)*. American Girl Publishing, Inc. (intermediate)
- Rotner, S. (2003). *Lots of Feelings*. Millbrook Press. (primary)

Storybooks Illustrating Various Emotions:

- Bunting, E. (1990). *The Wall*. Clarion Books. (intermediate)
- Frame, J. (2008). *Yesterday I Had the Blues*. Tricycle Press. (primary)
- Harper, J. (2004). *I Like Where I Am*. G.P. Putnam's Sons. (primary)
- Johnston, T. (2001). *Uncle Rain Cloud*. Charlesbridge Publishing. (intermediate)
- Kachenmeister, C. (2001). *On Monday When It Rained*. Sandpiper. (primary)
- Lugwig, T. (2005). *My Secret Bully*. Tricycle Press. (intermediate)
- Polaccio, P. (1994). *Pink and Say*. Philomel Books. (intermediate)
- Polaccio, P. (2001). *Thank You Mr. Falker*. Philomel Books. (primary–intermediate)

Feeling Happy:

- Aboff, E. (2010). *Everyone Feels Happy Sometimes (Everyone Has Feelings)*. Picture Window Books. (primary)
- Frost, H. (2000). *Feeling Happy (Emotions)*. Pebble Books. (primary)
- Barclay, J. (2002). *Going on a Journey to the Sea*. Lobster Press. (primary)
- Bertrand, D. (2004). *My Pal Victor*. Raven Tree Press. (primary, bilingual).
- Budd, E. (2000). *Glad: Thoughts and Feelings*. The Child's World, Inc. (primary–intermediate)
- Rylant, C. (2004). *The Relatives Came*. Live Oak Media. (primary–intermediate)
- Wilcox, B. (2001). *Hip, Hip Hooray for Annie McRae!* Clarion Books (primary)
- Wood, D. (2005). *The Secret of Saying Thanks*. Simon & Schuster. (intermediate)

Feeling Sad:

- Aboff, E. (2010). *Everyone Feels Sad Sometimes (Everyone Has Feelings)*. Picture Window Books. (primary)
- Apel, M. (2001). *Let's Talk about Feeling Lonely*. Powerkids. (primary)
- Berry, J. (2010). *Let's Talk about Feeling Sad*. Joy Berry Books. (primary)
- Berry, J. (2010). *Let's Talk about Feeling Disappointed*. Joy Berry Books. (primary)
- Danneberg, J. (2006). *Last Day Blues*. Charlesbridge. (primary–intermediate)
- Frost, H. (2000). *Feeling Sad (Emotions)*. Pebble Books. (primary)
- Goldblatt, R. (2004). *The Boy Who Didn't Want to be Sad*. Magination Press. (primary)
- Medina, S. (2007). *Lonely Feelings*. Heinemann-Raintree. (primary)
- Rosen, M. (2004). *Michael Rosen's Sad Book*. Candlewick Press. (intermediate)
- Viorst, J. (2009). *Alexander and the Terrible, Horrible, No Good, Very Bad Day*. Atheneum Books for Young Readers. (primary)

Feeling Angry:

- Aboff, E. (2010). *Everyone Feels Angry Sometimes (Everyone Has Feelings)*. Picture Window Books. (primary)
- Bang, M. (2004). *When Sophie Gets Angry–Really, Really Angry*. Scholastic. (primary)
- Berry, J. (2010). *Let's Talk about Feeling Angry*. Joy Berry Books. (primary)
- Berry, J. (2000). *Talk about Feeling Frustrated: A Personal Feelings Book*. Gold Star Books. (primary)
- Fox, L. (2000). *I Am So Angry I Could Scream: Helping Children Deal with Anger*. New Horizon Press. (primary–intermediate)
- Frost, H. (2000). *Feeling Angry*. Capstone Press. (primary)
- Kroll, S. (2002). *That Makes Me Mad*. SeaStar Books. (primary)

Feeling Scared:

- Aboff, E. (2010). *Everyone Feels Scared Sometimes (Everyone Has Feelings)*. Picture Window Books. (primary)
- Annunziata, J. (2009). *Sometimes I'm Scared*. Magination Press. (primary)
- Berry, J. (2010). *Let's Talk About Feeling Afraid*. Joy Berry Books. (primary)
- Berry, J. (2010). *Let's Talk About Feeling Worried*. Joy Berry Books. (primary)
- Braithwaite, A. (2002). *Feeling Scared (Choices)*. A&C Black Publishers Ltd. (primary)
- Frost, H. (2000). *Feeling Scared (Emotions)*. Pebble Books. (primary)
- Polacco, P. (1993). *Some Birthday*. Simon & Schuster. (primary)
- Powling, C. (2002). *The Kingfisher Book of Scary Stories*. Kingfisher. (intermediate)
- Shepherd, J. (2004). *What I Look Like When I Am Scared*. Powerkids Press. (primary)
- Wiesner, D. (2008). *Hurricane*. Houghton Mifflin. (primary–intermediate)

Feeling Surprised:

- Brown, M. (2004). *Arthur's Birthday Surprise*. LB Kids. (primary)
- Hughes, S. (2009). *Alfie and the Birthday Surprise*. Red Fox Reprint Edition. (primary)
- Rey, M. (2003). *Curious George and the Birthday Surprise*. HMH Books. (primary)
- Shepherd, J. (2004). *What I Look Like When I Am Surprised/Como Me Veo Cuando Estoy Sorprendido*. Buenas Letras. (primary, bilingual)

Feeling Disgusted:
- Pittau, F. (2004). *That's Disgusting.* Black Dog & Leventhal Publishers. (primary)
- Weintraub, A. (2005). *The Everything Kids' Gross Joke Book.* Adams Media. (primary–intermediate)

Feeling Embarrassed:
- Apel, M. (2001). *Let's Talk about Feeling Embarrassed.* Powerkid Press. (primary)
- Berry, J. (2000). *Let's Talk about Feeling Embarrassed: An Interpersonal Feelings Book.* Gold Star Publishing. (primary)
- Munsch, R. (2006). *I'm So Embarrassed.* Cartwheel Books. (primary)

Feeling Confused:
- Apel, M. (2001) *Let's Talk about Feeling Confused.* Rosen Publishing Group. (primary–intermediate)
- Randolph, J. (2004). *What I Look Like I Am Confused.* Rosen Publishing Group. (primary, bilingual)

Feeling Grumpy:
- Kurtz, J. (2007). *Rain Romp: Stomping Away a Grouchy Day.* Greenwillow Books. (primary)
- Lichtenheld, T. (2007). *What Are You So Grumpy About?* Little Brown Books for Young Readers. (intermediate)

Feeling Jealous:
- Berry, J. (2010). *Let's Talk about Feeling Jealous.* Joy Berry Books. (primary)
- Braithwaite, A. (2002). *Feeling Jealous (Choices).* A&C Black Publisher. (primary)
- Levete, S. (2008). *Feeling Jealous (Thoughts & Feelings).* Franklin Watts Ltd. (primary)

Feeling Shy:
- Berry, J. (2010). *Let's Talk About Feeling Shy.* Joy Berry Books. (primary)
- Braithwaite, A. (2001). *Feeling Shy (Choices).* A&C Black Publisher. (primary)
- Hewitt, S. (1999). *Feeling Shy (Feelings).* Franklin Watts Ltd. (primary)
- Johnston, M. (1998). *Let's Talk about Being Shy.* Hazelden Publishing. (primary)

How Would You Feel?

Read the following short scenarios (or make up your own) and have students tell how they would feel. It may also be helpful to act out these scenes, particularly for students with more limited verbal comprehension abilities.
- You lost your money.
- Another kid hit you for no reason.
- You are going to see a good movie.
- Your best friend is moving away.
- You hear noises in the middle of the night.
- The other kids won't let you play with them.
- Someone called you a bad name.

- You are playing video games with a good friend.
- You are going out for ice cream.
- Your dog was hit by a car.
- Someone stole your lunch money.
- You are going on a fun vacation.
- You are riding in the car and the car starts sliding off the road.
- You are going on a fieldtrip today.
- You tripped and fell while everyone was watching.
- You don't have anyone to play with.
- Your friend has lots of money to spend, but you don't have any.
- You made fun of your friend and made her cry.
- Your teacher gave you a worksheet, but you don't understand what to do.
- It is your first day at a new school and you don't know anyone.

Learning about Emotions through Acting

Short skits and plays, written at every reading level, are readily available and provide a great opportunity for students to explore different emotions. Activities and resources for demonstrating body language through acting are provided in Chapter 7, *Putting It All Together,* on pages 92-93. Some of these activities could be used to examine emotions by emphasizing how characters would feel.

Using Videos

Watch scenes from favorite movies, including enough of the video so the students understand what is happening in the story. Pause and discuss what the characters are feeling and why they feel that way. Point out facial expression cues, as needed. For example, say: "Look at her mouth. Is that a happy mouth?" (Throughout this book, scenes from age appropriate DVDs are listed, with scenes selected to illustrate different types of body language. These movie clips can be used to explore emotions as well.)

Free Online Resources

The Do2Learn website (www.do2learn.com) offers a number of free activities and materials for teaching about emotions, including worksheets, scenarios, and Emotions Check-In/Out.

Chapter 2

Facial Expressions

This curriculum does not provide extensive activities for teaching facial expressions, as there are other materials that focus exclusively on teaching students with disabilities about expressions. However, this chapter reviews the essentials and suggests resources and basic activities, and later chapters include activities that deal with expressions along with other types of body language. If you have students who need more work on recognizing expressions, you may wish to consult *Getting the Message: Learning to Read Facial Expressions.**

First Step: Seeing the Differences

Before beginning to teach different facial expressions, gather photos showing different expressions from magazines and the Internet. Have students note how the different parts of the face change, including the following:

- The eyes—wide open, squinting, downcast, looking up
- The eyebrows—neutral, up, down, or quick movements
- The mouth—neutral, smiling, frowning, tightly closed, open
- The head—tilted down, to the side, down and to the side, or upright
- Facial muscles—tensed or relaxed

Using photos or online resources (see resources below) have students guess the emotions associated with the different expressions. As well as offering an introduction to facial expressions, this activity provides an opportunity to see which expressions the student already understands.

The Basic Facial Expressions

When introducing facial expressions, begin with the six facial expressions that correspond with the six primary emotions:

1. *happiness,*
2. *sadness,*
3. *anger,*

---

* Pat Crissey, *Getting the Message: Learning to Read Facial Expressions* (Verona, WI: Attainment Company, 2007).

4. *fear,*

5. *surprise,* and

6. *disgust.*

Have students look for what makes a face appear happy, sad, angry, etc. See page 13 for photos showing the six basic expressions.

Activities for Teaching Facial Expressions

The following activities can be used to teach all facial expressions:

- Either purchase or create a set of facial expression cards. Cards can be created using photos from magazines, searching online for images (for example, Google/images), or taking photos of someone modeling different expressions. Photos can be glued on index cards and laminated for durability.
- Match and sort facial expressions cards according to the emotions they express.
- Play a game with the cards, having each student draw a card and imitate the expression, while other students try to guess the emotion.
- Have students draw a card and state a reason the person might be feeling that way (for example, looking angry because someone called him a name).
- Create a second set of cards depicting situations that might evoke different emotions, such as a picture of a birthday present, a melting snowman, or a growling dog. Have students match an expression to the corresponding situation.
- Create collages using faces to illustrate different emotions. For example, create a happy face or sad face collage.
- Write feeling words on slips of paper or index cards and have players draw a card. Then play charades, with one player making a facial expression that goes with the feeling word drawn, while other players try to guess. Simple line drawings, such as a smiley face, could be added to the word cards for students who may have difficulty reading text.

Facial Expression Lotto

Reprinted from: Pat Crissey, *Getting the Message* (Verona, WI: Attainment Company, 2007).

- Play facial expressions lotto. Create a set of boards, so each player has a unique board with a different arrangement of pictures of facial expressions. (See example at left.) Use a set of feeling word cards, as described for playing charades above. Draw the top word card from the pile and read the feeling aloud. Players then place markers, such as pennies or poker chips, on a facial expression that illustrates the named emotion. The first player to cover three pictures in a row wins.
- Have students draw simple cartoon faces showing different emotions.
- Have students recall an emotional situation, then make the associated facial expression while looking in a mirror.
- Find examples of facial expressions in picture books. Read the story and discuss how the characters are feeling.
- Watch clips from videos, pausing to note facial expressions.
- Look for examples of facial expressions in real life—in the classroom or in family situations. Explain to students that it could be considered rude to stare at or comment about facial expressions of strangers in the community.

Expressing Different Emotional Intensity

Once the student recognizes basic facial expressions, she's ready to discriminate how the face changes to reflect different intensities of those emotions. For example, a face may express that the person is feeling slightly irritated or completely enraged. Demonstrate or look at examples of how facial expressions change as the intensity of an emotion increases. Relate different emotional intensities to situations that lead to those feelings. The following descriptive words may help clarify different intensities of the basic emotions.

1. Happiness: satisfied, pleased, cheerful, happy, delighted, overjoyed, ecstatic
2. Sadness: disappointed, unhappy, sad, sorrowful, distressed, miserable, inconsolable
3. Anger: bothered, offended, irritated, upset, angry, furious, enraged
4. Fear: uneasy, worried, anxious, fearful, alarmed, scared, terrified
5. Surprise: taken aback, surprised, astonished
6. Disgust: squeamish, disgusted, repelled, revolted

Other Common Facial Expressions

There is virtually an endless variety of different facial expressions. The ones listed below are common expressions that are important for most students to know, but choose those expressions that best meet your students' needs.

- Interested
- Bored
- Contemptuous
- Embarrassed
- Shy
- Confident/proud
- Sorry/ashamed
- Confused
- Jealous
- Doubtful
- Sincere smile
- Polite/insincere smile

Facial expressions can be confusing. Not every emotion has a distinct facial expression, so students always need to take context into account when trying to decipher the meaning of an expression. A variety of activities throughout this curriculum offer practice at using context along with body language to understand nonverbal communication.

Resources for Teaching Facial Expressions

- *Getting the Message: Learning to Read Facial Expressions* by Pat Crissey (Attainment Company, 2007).
- The Do2Learn website (www.do2learn.com) offers a number of free activities and materials for teaching about facial expressions, including *The Feelings Game* and *Facial Expressions Program*.

- YouTube provides many examples of facial expressions. Search under "facial expressions tutorial" or "facial expressions and autism" to find some helpful videos. "Facial Expressions Tutorial by Khappucino" illustrates and describes how the face differs in nine of the most common expressions.
- There are numerous "facial expressions tests" online. Search and find one appropriate for your students.
- A free app, called *ABA Emotions Flash Cards,* is available for iPhone, iPod Touch, and iPad at www.kindergarten.com.

Basic Facial Expressions

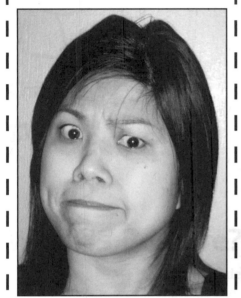

Angry

Happy

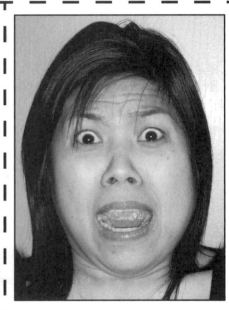

Scared

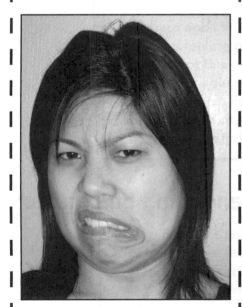

Disgusted

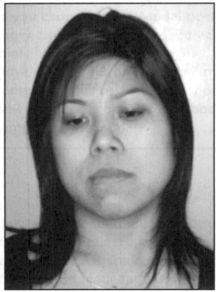

Sad

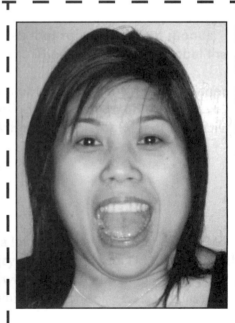

Surprised

Model and Practice

Tell students that you are going to demonstrate the same posture two times, but there will be something different between the two postures. Model the same posture first relaxed, then tense. (Make sure the posture and your facial expressions remain basically the same, although your body will be rigid and your hands can be clenched when demonstrating the tense posture.) Ask students to tell what is different.

Write the word "tense" on the board. Ask a volunteer to model a tense posture and have students describe what a tense body looks like (clenched fists, body looks tight or stiff) and write these observations on the board.

Ask students to give examples of times or reasons that someone would be tense, such as when they are frightened, angry, frustrated, or cold. Point out that generally the more tense the body is, the more scared, angry, frustrated, or cold the person probably is feeling.

Write the word "relaxed" on the board and repeat the previous activities.

Help students feel what tension is by demonstrating tensing and relaxing the following body parts, having students imitate your actions:

- hands,
- arms,
- shoulders,
- face.

Have students demonstrate tense and relaxed postures, taking turns looking at themselves in the mirror.

 # Worksheet—Relaxed and Tense Postures #1

Distribute the "Relaxed and Tense Postures #1" worksheet (#3-1 in the Activity pages in the Appendix). Ask students to write descriptions of what each posture looks like (loose, easy going, tight, rigid) and the feelings associated with it (angry, scared, OK, excited).

Struggling writers could copy from the board, or draw simple pictures of the body to show tension or relaxation. They could draw simple faces to tell what the person is feeling or cut and glue the facial expression cartoons (Appendix 3-2).

Copy and distribute the "Name the Posture—Tense or Relaxed #1" worksheet (Appendix 3-3) and have students name the posture in each picture. This activity could be done as a group or students could work in pairs, matching struggling readers with more proficient readers.

 # Treasure Hunt

Pass out old magazines, comics, greeting cards, etc. and have students search for and cut out examples of people looking tense and relaxed. Have individuals share their pictures and tell why the person looks tense or relaxed. Save the pictures for future activities.

Open and Closed Postures

When a person is feeling threatened or upset, he will adopt a closed, or defensive posture, pulling the body together, making it appear smaller. Arms may be crossed over the chest, shoulders hunched, legs close together or tightly crossed, if seated.

An open posture reflects a relaxed, receptive mood. The posture is upright, shoulders erect, legs and arms not pulled tightly into or around the body.

Model and Practice

Ask for volunteers to stand up and model what they think is an open and a closed posture. Then provide models for these postures, either modeling the posture yourself or pointing out students who are correctly modeling the posture. Have students take turns practicing the postures in front of a full-length mirror. Ask students to describe how each posture makes them feel. Does it make them feel tense, relaxed, excited, angry, scared, cold, etc.?

Worksheets—Open and Closed Postures

Distribute and complete "Open and Closed Postures #2" (Appendix 3-4), which shows standing postures.

Repeat with "Open and Closed Postures #3" (Appendix 3-5), which shows open and closed sitting postures.

Then distribute and complete "Name the Posture—Open & Closed #2" (Appendix 3-6, page 111).

Point out that the position of the *arms* is more important when determining whether someone is tense or relaxed. With leg positions, look for tension, rather than open or closed positions, as an open position can be aggressive, while crossed legs may be very relaxed. Ask students how individuals appear to feel when in open and closed postures and write the related emotion words under each posture. (See list below.)

Closed Posture	Open Posture
angry	relaxed
bored	interested
afraid	happy
doubtful	neutral
cold	glad
bothered	pleased
frustrated	proud
shy	confident
confused	
sorry	

Show What You're Thinking

Have all or a selected number of students stand while you read some thoughts. Direct the standing students to show what their posture would be like if they were having that thought. See the suggested list of thoughts below. Repeat the activity with students seated.

Thoughts
"It's freezing in here."
"I'm tired of standing here in line."
"It's fun watching the game."
"This is so boring."
"That really makes me mad!"
"I don't like it when he says that."
"She's wrong!"
"He's a pretty cool guy."
"It's OK. I'll just wait here."
"I don't want to talk to these people."

Treasure Hunt

Have students look through magazines or books to find pictures of individuals standing or sitting, showing open and closed postures. They may be able to use pictures found in the previous treasure hunt.

Expanded and Slumped Postures

Expanded postures are open postures, but more so. Arms are extended, the chest is expanded, and the body is erect. This posture can express confidence, excitement, or aggression.

Slumped postures are the opposite. The body seems to shrink, as if the person is trying to disappear. The body is hunched over, the head is down, with the arms close to the body. This posture is associated with feeling sad, ashamed, or frightened.

Model and Practice

Write the word "expanded" on the board and ask students if they know what it means. (For younger students, the expression "stretched out" or "very open" could be used instead.) If helpful, have a student look up the word expanded in the dictionary and read the definition.

Ask students to model what they think might be an expanded posture. Point out student examples or model the posture yourself, with your arms stretched out either above your head or to the side, and your head up. Direct attention to the position of the head and arms as well as the erect posture. Have students imitate the posture, looking at themselves in the mirror.

Ask students to describe the posture (arms stretched out, head up) and how they feel when standing that way. Write the emotion words on the board. (See list below.)

Ask students to model what they think would be the opposite of an expanded posture. Write the word "slumped" on the board. Demonstrate and point out the position of the head and arms. Model different examples of slumped postures, both sitting and standing. Then have students imitate these postures or come up with their own, looking at themselves in the mirror.

Ask students to describe slumped postures and how they feel when taking these postures. Write the emotion words on the board.

Expanded	Slumped
very happy	troubled
excited	hopeless
proud	defeated
terrific	discouraged
thrilled	depressed
ecstatic	miserable
exhilarated	rejected
conceited	desolate
arrogant	grieving
	lonely

Worksheets—Expanded and Slumped Postures

Distribute and complete the worksheets "Expanded and Slumped Postures #4 and #5" (Appendix 3-7 and 3-8) and "Name the Posture—Expanded & Slumped #3" (Appendix 3-9).

Show What You're Thinking

With the thoughts below, repeat the "Show What You're Thinking" activity from above, having the students use expanded and slumping postures. (Students may include open and closed positions as part of their postures.)

Thoughts
"Oh! You surprised me!"
"I'm so tired."
"This has been a lousy day."
"Yeah! Our team won!"
"Oh, wow! What a great surprise!"
"Go away and leave me alone."
"I don't know what to do."
"I did it! I did it!"
"I'm feeling really down today."
"Ah! The sun feels so good."

Treasure Hunt

Have students look through books and magazines to find pictures showing individuals in expanded and slumped postures. They may be able to use some of the pictures found in previous treasure hunts.

Expanded—Slumped Posture Scale

Using butcher paper or the board, draw a scale that says "expanded" on one end and "slumped" on the other end. Have students use pictures to create their own scale, or work together in groups. Use pictures collected in the Treasure Hunt activity.

Leaning Postures—Towards or Away

In general, people tend to lean towards others when they are interested in what the person is saying or to express aggression. They lean away when they are feeling disinterested, resistant, or intimidated. This can be confusing for people with autism or others who have difficulties interpreting social cues, as there can be a subtle difference between interest versus aggression. That is why it is essential to teach students to also look at whether the posture is open, closed, or expanded.

It may be necessary to explain to some students how others typically view a posture. For example, you may need to point out that when a person is leaning away, with a closed posture, others generally think the person is not interested or is resisting what is being said.

Model and Practice

Select students to model the following postures for the class. Then ask students to pair up and practice the following postures.

- facing each other—leaning towards the other person
- facing each other—leaning away from the other person
- side by side—leaning towards
- side by side—leaning away

Have students combine open, closed, and expanded positions with leaning postures by practicing the postures below. Point out that if someone leans forward with an expanded posture, he looks threatening, as if he is trying to look bigger and not afraid.

Ask students how each posture makes them feel and how others look like they feel when they take that posture.

- Leaning towards with open posture (interested, in agreement, pleased)
- Leaning towards with closed posture (angry, disagreement)
- Leaning towards with an expanded posture (aggressive)
- Leaning away with open posture (listening, interested, considering, thinking)
- Leaning away with closed posture (lack of interest, bored, angry, pouting, shy, fearful)

Worksheets—Towards and Away Worksheets

Distribute and complete copies of the following worksheets:

- "Towards and Away Postures #6" (Appendix 3-10)
- "Learning Towards #7" (3-11)
- "Towards and Away Postures #8" (3-12)
- "Name the Posture—Towards & Away #4" (3-13)

Depending on your students' ages and abilities, have them complete the worksheets individually or in groups. If students have difficulties understanding what emotions are depicted, have two students model the postures shown in the worksheets.

Treasure Hunt

Have students find pictures of postures of individuals who are leaning towards or away from other people. They may be able to use some of the pictures found in the previous treasure hunts.

Additional Learning Activities

 ## What Are They Feeling? Worksheets

Distribute and complete the following worksheets:
- "How Are They Feeling? #1" (Appendix 3-14)
- "How Are They Feeling? #2" (3-15)
- "How Are They Feeling? #3" (3-16)
- "What Are They Thinking? #4" (3-17)

 ## Looking Confident

Discuss the meaning of the word "confidence" and how someone looks confident (standing erect, open posture). Have students practice a confident posture, looking at themselves in the mirror. Then have them look scared or frightened (slumped over, leaning away and closed).

Discuss why it's important to look confident. (You're less likely to be picked on or bullied, people respect you more, and it can actually make you feel more confident.)

Play the "Confidence Game." Tell students that at random times throughout the day, you will say, "Look confident" or another similar cue, and everyone is to assume a confident posture, regardless of how they may be actually feeling. Point out students who look particularly confident, noting what it is about their posture that makes them look confident.

 ## Walking the Walk

Write the following words on the board: confident, scared, sad, relaxed, and angry. Then ask students to watch as you walk and note how they think you are feeling. Demonstrate various postures as you walk, such as walking in a relaxed, open posture and in a tense, slumped posture.

Write the following walking styles on the board or on cards. Have students model them while other students say how it looks like the person is feeling.

- relaxed & expanded
- slumped & slow
- fast & open
- fast & tense
- tense & closed
- slow & closed
- fast & closed
- slow & relaxed
- tense & slow
- slumped & tense

Emotion Walk

Create a set of cards ahead of time with emotion words written on them, such as: happy, sad, angry, scared, shy, embarrassed, surprised, tired, bored, confused, and ashamed.

Choose one person to be the leader. All of the other players begin walking around in a typical manner.

The leader then draws one of the cards and reads it aloud. Everyone will begin walking as if they are feeling that emotion. After a few seconds, the leader calls out, "Freeze!" Everyone freezes their posture and students observe each other's postures. The leader then draws another card and the game continues.

Act It Out—Postures

Have students act out the short role plays from Appendix 3-18, or use other short scenes from plays. While students rehearse their role plays, coach them to use body postures to express what they would be feeling. The following are the most likely postures to be displayed in the role plays, though different interpretations may be valid.

- Role play #1: actor #1—expanded; actor #2—closed and slumped
- Role play #2: actor #1—towards and open: actor #2—slumped
- Role play #3: actors #1 and #2—open and towards
- Role play #4: actor #1—open and towards: actor #2—closed and away
- Role play #5: actor #1—towards, expanded, and tense: #2—away and open
- Role play #6: actor #1—closed and tense: actor #2—relaxed and open

As students perform, have them "freeze" at different times and ask others to identify the emotion and corresponding body posture. An alternative would be to videotape the role plays, pausing the video at different points, to discuss the body postures and implied emotions.

Candid Camera

Take photos of students as they go through their daily activities. At a later time, look over the photos, either individually or in a group, and describe the different postures seen.

Posture Poses

Take photos of students posing in different postures. Have prints commercially made or print them out on your computer printer. Label postures and display.

Sunday Funnies

Place copies of cartoons or comic strips on an overhead projector or call up one of the websites below on an interactive whiteboard and have students point out the various postures. Use one of the following comic strips or other personal favorites. Archives of comics can usually be found on the comic strip's website.

- Peanuts—www.unitedmedia.com/comics/peanuts
- Stan 'n' Isaac—www.stan-isaac.com
- Calvin and Hobbes—www.gocomics.com/calvinandhobbes
- Garfield—www.garfield.com
- Grand Avenue—comics.com/comics/grandave/index.html
- Luann—www.luannsroom.com
- Zits—www.kingfeatures.com/features/comics/comics.html

Stop Action

Play short segments of DVDs or videos with the sound turned off. Hit pause and have students point out the different postures they see when characters are standing, sitting, and walking.

Mask Charades

Write the short scenarios below on individual cards, or create your own. Place the cards in a bag or box or place them face down and have students take turns drawing a card.

The student who drew the card then places a mask over his or her face and shows what he or she is feeling using body posture while other students try to guess the emotion.

Write the list of emotions on the board for students to choose from. (A mask is used so that students must use their body and not their face to display the emotion. A template for making a simple mask can be found in Appendix 3-19.)

Scenarios
It's time for your favorite TV show. You feel **happy.**
You can't go to the movie because your parent has to work. You feel **sad.**
You're walking home alone and you think someone is following you. You feel **scared.**
Another kid keeps calling you names. You feel **angry.**
You just found out you won 1st prize. You feel **excited!**
Your friend is going to tell you a big secret. You feel **interested.**
You are watching a really boring movie. You feel **bored.**
The teacher called on you and you weren't listening. Everyone looked at you. You feel **embarrassed.**
You don't think it's fair that the teacher never calls on you. You feel **bothered.**
All of a sudden your friend jumps out and surprises you. You feel **surprised**.

Cartoon Figures

Teaching students how to draw cartoon figures can help them learn about body postures. The following books are useful resources.

- Bulloch, Ivan (1998). *Cartoons & Animations.* Children's Press.
- Gair, Angela (1991). *How to Draw and Paint People.* Wellfleet Press.
- Gray, Peter (2006). *Drawing Manga Female Action Figures* and *Drawing Manga Male Action Figures.* PowerPlus Books.
- Hart, Christopher (2004). *Kids Draw Manga.* Watson-Guptill Publications.
- Mayne, Don (2000). *Draw Your Own Cartoons!* Williamson Publishing.
- Roche, Art (2005). *Art for Kids: Cartooning.* Larks Books.

Flip Book Animation

Make copies of Flipbook Pictures (Appendix 3-20) and have students color as desired and cut along the dotted line. Have students use their pencil to curl the top page as shown on the directions, then roll the pencil and page back and forth quickly to see the figure change his posture.

If desired, have students draw figures to create their own flipbook pictures. A great resource for creating different types of animations is *Animation: How to Draw Your Own Flipbooks and Other Fun Ways to Make Cartoons Move* by Patrick Jenkins.

Dictionary of Body Postures

Have students use the pictures they collected in the treasure hunt activities to create a dictionary. Glue each picture on a sheet of paper and give it a title that tells how the person in the picture is feeling. Place sheets together in a binder, putting them in alphabetical order.

Memory Game ~ Postures

Have students stand in a circle in neutral, relaxed postures. The first player takes a posture, holds it for two seconds, and then returns to a neutral posture. The next student then copies the first posture, then makes up another posture, and holds it for two seconds. Play continues around the circle, with each successive student adding a new posture until students are unable to remember all the postures in order.

Read, Pause, and Pose

Read aloud a story that involves a variety of actions and emotions. Pause at points in the story where the character or characters would likely be taking a particular posture. Ask students to demonstrate these postures. When first using this activity, use picture books and show the students the illustrations, then have students model the postures. Once students become adept at this, have students display the postures before showing them the illustration.

Read, Pause, and Draw

Follow the directions for "Read, Pause, and Pose," except instead of having students take poses, have students draw pictures of the characters as they would appear in the story.

Activity Pages

Make copies of "Body and Face Match-up" and "Read the Scene—Posture" Appendix 3-21 and 3-22, for students to complete. If students have trouble completing the worksheets, draw attention to the postures and expressions of the people in the illustrations.

Unit Quiz: Posture

Have students take the quiz in Appendix 3-23 independently, or together as a group.

Chapter 4

Body Orientation and Eye Gaze

Body orientation refers to the position of the body in reference to others. For example, when someone turns her body, or the upper part of her body, so it is facing another person, this is generally interpreted to mean that she is interested and listening. Eye gaze refers to what the person is looking at, which also implies interest. (This is different from eye contact, in which one person looks into the eyes of another person who is returning the gaze.) Both body orientation and eye gaze can be difficult for students with certain disabilities, since they may not understand what is being communicated through these types of body language.

What Is Body Orientation?

Copy and cut out the "Body Pointing Figures" (Appendix 4-1). Place set #1 of the cutout figures on a board, so they are facing each other. Ask the students:

- Do both boys look interested in talking with each other?
- How can you tell?

Remove the figure of Roy from the board and replace it with the figure of Roy from set #2.

- Do both boys look interested now?
- Why not?
- What could Roy be saying with his body? (He's not interested in what Jake is saying. He doesn't know Jake is talking to him. He's mad at Jake.)

Place the figures on the board in different ways. (Roy facing Jake, with Jake turned away. Both boys turned away from each other.) Ask students what the different positions could mean.

Body Pointing

 Model and Practice

Pair up students and have them take positions facing each other, then have them alternately turn away from the other person. Ask them:

- Do you feel like you could talk to the other person when she's facing you?
- Does she seem interested?

- What about when she turns away?

Write the words "body pointing" on the board. Explain that body pointing is turning your body, particularly your upper body (face and shoulders), so that it is facing the other person. With older students the term "body orientation" could be introduced.

Create a Chart

Draw a T-chart on the board or a large sheet of paper, with the word "towards" written on one side and "away" on the other. Ask students to tell what it could mean when someone has his or her body pointing towards another person and write their responses on the chart. Do the same for turning the body away. See example below.

Understanding Body Pointing	
Towards	Away
• paying attention • interested • agree with speaker • like the person	• not paying attention • not interested • disagree, angry, or upset • finished talking, need to go • don't know person is talking to him or her

Copies could be made of the blank "Understanding Body Pointing" chart, Appendix 4-3, for students to use to copy the responses.

Friendly Body Pointing

Ask one student to come stand in front of the class while the other students observe. Explain that you are going to talk with this student, using two different positions. You want the student you are talking to and the rest of the class to look for differences in body pointing.

First, stand so that you are facing the student directly, observing proper personal space. Talk to the student about any informal, friendly topic.

Next, stand to the side of the student at a 45-degree angle, with your head turned towards her. Talk to the student in the same manner as above. Next, ask her:

- Did it feel different when I was standing right in front of you than when I stood off to your side? If so, how?
- How did it look to others? (Conversations are viewed as more serious when face-to-face, and friendlier when standing at an angle.)

Explain that a person will usually stand directly facing the other person when:

- She has something important to say to that person, such as asking an important question, asking permission, telling about something that is wrong, etc.
- When talking about something private and she doesn't want others to join the conversation.

• When she is mad or is being aggressive or confrontational.

Standing at an angle feels friendlier and more informal to most people.

Pair up students and have them practice these positions. You may want to suggest friendly topics for them to talk about, such as favorite TV shows, weekend plans, etc.

Measuring Angles

This activity is for students who have some basic understanding of geometry and angles.

• Place butcher paper on the floor for students to stand on or use masking tape.
• Have two students stand so they feel comfortable talking with each other.
• Have another student place a ruler in front of each student's toes and draw a line on the butcher paper or place a piece of masking tape on the floor next to the ruler.
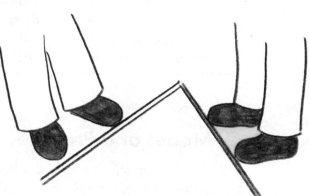
• Extend the lines until they meet and then measure the angle. Is it appropriately a 45° angle? (See illustration at right.)
• Try this with different pairs of students.

Who Can I Talk To?

Ask for five volunteers. Have two of them stand facing each other directly and pretend to be talking about something important and private. Have another two volunteers stand at a 45 degree angle to one another and pretend to be having a friendly conversation. Tell the remaining volunteer that she is alone at a party and wants to talk to someone. Which group would she try to join and why? If necessary, explain which group *you* would join and why.

Then ask the pair what they can do to include the other person in their conversation (look at the new person, possibly turn their body more towards her).

Worksheets—Reading the Scene—Body Pointing

Have students complete the two "Read the Scene" worksheets (Appendix 4-4 and 4-5). Review the answers and discuss what could be happening in the picture and the body language clues.

Eye Gaze

What Is Eye Gaze?

Make copies of the "Eye Gaze Faces" activity (Appendix 4-6) and cut them out. Place set #1 of the cutout faces on a board, so they are facing each other. Ask the students:

- Do both girls look interested in talking with each other?
- How can you tell?

Write the term "eye gaze" on the board and explain that it means what you are looking at. People point to what they are interested in with their eyes as well as their bodies.

- Remove the face of Emma from the board and replace it with the face of Emma from set #2.
- Do both girls look interested now?
- Why not?
- What could Emma be saying with her eye gaze? (She's interested in something else. She doesn't know Jenny is talking to her. She's mad at Jenny.)

Place the faces on the board so that Emma and Jenny are looking different ways and ask students to guess what might be going on.

Model and Practice

Pair up students and ask them to take positions looking at each other, then have student #1 look away from student #2. Then switch roles. Ask the students:

- Do you feel like you could talk to the other person when she's looking at you?
- Does she seem interested?
- What about when she looks away?

Divide students into small groups of two to four students and have them all sit with their backs to each other. Assign each group a topic to talk about, such as what they did over the weekend, and have them talk to each other for two minutes without turning and looking at each other.

Discuss how it felt to talk to each other without being able to see each other or being able to make eye contact.

Have the same groups of students turn their chairs around and discuss the same topic for two minutes. Discuss how it felt this time.

Worksheets—Reading the Scene—Eye Gaze

Have students complete the two "Read the Scene" worksheets in Appendix 4-7 and 4-8. Review the answers and discuss what could be happening in the pictures and what clues students use to determine what might be happening.

Looking at Others—When and how much?

Discuss eye gaze with the following or similar questions.

- What does it mean to have "eye contact" with someone?
- When do people give eye contact?
  - ○ When someone is talking to them or they are talking with someone or when they want to get someone's attention. Usually people wait until they are physically close to a person before making eye contact, unless they are trying to signal the person.
- When you are giving eye contact, how long do you look at the person's eyes?
  - ○ Only for a few seconds, then you look away, then look back. Explain that when someone looks at another's eyes, it is "on-and-off," or a series of glances—look briefly, look away, look briefly, etc. The average gaze length is just shy of three seconds, and only about one second when it's a mutual gaze.
- What do people think if you don't look at the person you are talking with?
  - ○ You're not interested or not listening,
  - ○ you're not telling the truth,
  - ○ you're shy, or
  - ○ you're being disrespectful.
- What do people think if you look at another's face too much or you stare at the person?
  - ○ You're angry or trying to bully.
  - ○ You are flirting with the person.
  - ○ You think there's something odd about the way they look.
- When you're talking with someone, how much of the time should you spend looking at the person?
  - ○ A little over half of the time, more when you are listening than when you are talking. According to Michael Argyle, a leading researcher in nonverbal communication, the average amount a person gazes at his or her conversation partner is 61 percent of the time overall; consisting of 41 percent of the time when talking and 75 percent of the time when listening.

Video Clips

The following are some video clips, available on DVD, that can be used to illustrate body orientation and eye gaze. To make it easier to locate the relevant scenes, the scene number is given, and often the number of minutes and seconds into the movie or scene. For example, Scene #7, at 00:00:22, means 22 seconds into scene #7. Further explanation about how to use video clips is given on page 97, "Using Video Clips."

- *Uncle Nino*—Scene #7, at 00:00:22. What does Bones communicate when he switches his eye gaze from Bobby to Joey? (That he doesn't believe what Bobby said.)

- *Cheaper by the Dozen*—Scene #12 from 00:37:05—0037:38. What does Hank want when he looks at his girlfriend? (He wants her to confirm or agree with what he is saying.) Why do the two girls look at each other after Hank says, "It's getting so I can hardly go out in public anymore?" (To express disbelief.)

Create a Chart

Draw a chart with three columns on the board or on a large sheet of paper. Ask students what they think it means when:

1. Someone looks at another person,
2. looks away or down, and
3. gives too much eye contact

Write their responses on the chart. Students could also write the responses on copies of the "Understanding Eye Contact" chart (Appendix 4-9).

Understanding Eye Contact		
Looks at other person	Looks away or down	Too much looking
• want to communicate • interested • to see reaction • feeling comfortable • want listener to understand • like talking to person • agree with person	• taking time to think • not interested • feeling shy, ashamed, or embarrassed • don't want to talk about topic • want to end conversation • not telling the truth • need to leave	• angry • trying to bully • don't know they are doing it • flirting

Follow the Gaze Game

Explain that you can often tell what someone is thinking about or interested in by looking at where that person is looking.

Play a game by pairing up students and have them sit facing each other. Player #1 then selects and looks at an object or person in the room. Player #2 tries to guess what player #1 is looking at.

Follow the Gaze Treasure Hunt

Have students search for pictures in old magazines or picture books to find pictures showing individuals looking at objects or other people. Students could then draw an arrow from the eyes to what the person is looking at.

It's Your Turn to Talk

Ask for a student volunteer or have another staff member join you in front of the class. Ask the class to watch and to see if they can tell when you are giving a signal that it is the other person's turn to talk. Carry on a brief conversation with several conversational exchanges, giving clear indications when it's the other person's turn to talk. (See list below.) Also glance off to the side while you are talking. (This is a common signal that you are not finished with what you're saying.) An alternative would be to videotape this conversation ahead of time. Show it first to students without pausing, then replay it, pausing to observe the conversational signals.

Ask students what they observed and explain how we signal it's the other person's turn to talk by:

- pausing,
- turning your head towards and looking at the person,
- sometimes raising your eyebrows (the eyebrow flash will be further discussed in gestures unit).

Point out that when the speaker glances off to the side, this usually indicates that he or she is not finished speaking.

Pair up students and have them practice talking to each other, making appropriate eye contact and looking at each other to signal it's the other's turn to talk. (Give topics or scripts if needed. Sample conversation scripts are provided in Appendix 4-10). Switch groups and repeat the activity. After each interval, ask students to rate themselves on the following:

- Did I give on-and-off eye contact?
- Did I pause and give eye contact when I was finished saying something or asking a question?

Alert! This Conversation Is Coming to an End

 ## Model and Practice

Explain to students that when people are having a conversation, they usually give signals that they are about to end the conversation before it actually happens. Tell students that you are going to model a conversation and give signals when you are about to end the conversation and ask them to note what they observe.

Ask one student to come up to be your conversational partner or have another staff person take that role. Briefly talk to that person about any topic. After a few seconds, begin to use the following signals that the conversation is ending by:

- glancing away from your conversational partner;
- saying something like, "It was good talking with you";
- and finally saying, "It's time to get on with the class," or "Thanks. You can take your seat now."

An alternative would be to videotape this conversation ahead of time. Show it first to students without pausing, and then replay it, pausing to observe the signals that the conversation is coming to an end.

Ask the observers what they saw. Write the answers on the board. Students could write observations on individual copies of the "Ending a Conversation" charts (Appendix 4-11).

Ending a Conversation		
Signals	What does it mean?	What do I do?
• look away from other person	• not interested or ending conversation	• change topic, ask a question, get ready to end conversation
• look at watch or clock	• may need to go	• be ready to end conversation
• look towards door	• getting ready to go	• end conversation
• ending statements: "I better get going"	• ending conversation	• end conversation
• turn body away from other person	• ending conversation	• end conversation
• move away from person	• ending conversation	• end conversation
• walk away	• ending conversation	• end conversation

Role Plays—Ending a Conversation

Copy and distribute the short role plays in Appendix 4-12. Pair up students and have them act out "Role Play #1," following the prompts written in the script. Switch roles and repeat.

Then have pairs of students act out "Role Play #2" several times, rotating the roles. Ask for volunteers to perform the role plays for the class.

I Got the Message. Now What?

Ask for a student volunteer to role-play a short scene with you in front of the class. The student needs to talk to you about a topic of her choice. While she is talking, look away for a few seconds, then turn and walk away without saying anything.

- What was I saying by looking away?
  - I wasn't interested or wanted to end the conversation.
- What could you (the speaker) do when I did that?
  - Change topic or ask a question when your conversation partner starts looking away.
  - When the person walks away, say, "Well, I'll see you later."
- What was I saying by walking away?
  - I wasn't interested, I was upset, I needed or wanted to go somewhere, or I couldn't get a word in edgewise.
- Was just walking away a good way to end the conversation?
  - No. It was rude.
- What could I have done instead?
  - I could have nodded my head, put a hand up to indicate stop, looked away, and said, "I need to go now. See you later."

- When you are talking and someone indicates that she wants or needs to go, what should you do?
  - Stop talking, let them go, and say, "I'll see you later."

Pair up students and have them take turns being the speaker and the listener who wants to leave. Practice the following:
- What to do when you are talking and the listener is looking away.
- What you can say and do if you don't have time or don't want to listen.

Homework Assignment

Give students an assignment of watching and seeing how others end a conversation. The assignment could be carried out at school, at home, in the community, or even on TV. Have students report back on what they observed, either as a written or verbal assignment.

Additional Learning Activities

Take Your Places

Collect pictures from storybooks or scenes from movies that illustrate body orientation or eye gaze. Then have students replicate the scene by having each student take the same posture and position as a person in the scene. Other students observe and see if the postures and orientations are correct.

Candid Camera

Take photos of students as they go through their daily activities. At a later time, look over the photos and have students point out the different body orientations and eye gaze.

Posed Pictures

Take photos of students modeling different body orientations and eye gaze. Discuss the body language in the photos. More advanced students could make up scenarios to explain what is happening in each photo.

Snapshot Scenarios

Pair up students and give each pair a snapshot scenario from the list in Appendix 4-13. Tell students that they are going to pretend that they are in the situation presented in the scenario and that someone took a photograph.

Write all the scenarios on the board or show them on an overhead projector or interactive whiteboard. Have each group demonstrate their "snapshot" while the rest of the class guesses which scenario they are showing. Discuss what might be happening and how the people in the snapshot might be feeling.

I Spy Lotto Game

Make copies of the lotto card template in Appendix 4-14. Write words in random order on the lotto cards to indicate different people or items in the classroom. Then write each of the words on a separate index card. Pictures could be used in addition to words for students who have difficulty reading. (See example below.)

The teacher takes the role of caller and draws a card, and, without showing the card, looks at the person or item written on the card. Each player then covers that space on their lotto board. The teacher continues to draw cards until a player wins the game. Students could also take turns being the caller.

Talk Show

Watch recorded segments from TV talk shows and observe how the interviewer and guests orient their bodies towards each other. (Playing the segment with the sound off may help students focus more on the body language.)

Have students pair up and interview each other. Either have students write down what questions to ask ahead of time or provide them with questions to ask.

Have the students perform for class or videotape them and then review.

Sunday Funnies

Make copies of cartoons or comic strips, place them on the overhead, and have students point out body orientation and eye gaze. See the list of comic strips on page 24.

Stop Action

Play short segments of DVDs with the sound turned off. Hit pause and have students point out examples of body orientation and eye gaze.

Read, Pause, and Pose

Follow the directions for the "Read, Pause, and Pose" activity, as described on page 25. Have students demonstrate orientation and eye gaze in addition to posture.

Read, Pause, and Draw

Follow the directions for "Read, Pause, and Draw," on page 26. Have students include orientation and eye gaze in their drawings of story characters.

Interview a Famous Person

Have students research a famous historical person and make up questions about that person to be answered during an interview. Pair up students and have them exchange their lists of questions, so the interviewer will have a list of questions to ask. Students will then take turns playing the role of the interviewer and famous person.

Activity Pages

Make copies of the following activity pages from Appendices 4-15, 4-16, 4-17, and 4-18:
- "What's Happening?"
- "What Are They Looking At?"
- "Tell What's Going On"
- "Reading Body Language"

Have the students complete the activities, alone or in groups.

End of Unit Quiz

Have the students complete "Unit Quiz—Body Pointing and Eye Gaze" in Appendix 4-19.

Chapter 5

Personal Space and Touching

Introduction—Personal Space Zones

After extensive research, anthropologist Edward T. Hall wrote about four distinct zones of comfort related to interpersonal interactions experienced by those living in the United States. [The zones are different for those living in Mexico, Central America, and South America.] In his book, *The Hidden Dimension,** he describes the following zones:

- *The Intimate Zone,* 0-18 inches or 0-45 centimeters, is reserved for close personal relationships. In this zone people hug or embrace and whisper or talk very quietly. Highly personal topics are discussed in this zone.

- *The Personal Zone,* 18 inches to 4 feet or 45 to 120 centimeters, is used when people are talking with close friends, classmates, and family members. Most everyday conversations are carried out in this zone. A normal speaking voice is used in this zone.

- *The Social Zone,* 4 feet to 12 feet or 1.25 to 3.5 meters, is used for talking with someone who is a stranger or not well known. People speak loudly enough to be heard in this zone. No personal or private matters are discussed in this zone.

- *The Public Zone,* 12 feet or 3.5 meters and further, is reserved for public speaking, such as participating in a discussion or giving a report. Conversations are not carried on in this zone. Most one-to-one communication is generally carried on through gestures until the social zone is entered.

These zones have been simplified in this book for teaching purposes. This chapter discusses:

- an individual's personal space bubble or "personal bubble" (less than 2 feet or 60 centimeters),
- the "talking zone" (approximately between 2 and 6 feet, or 60 and 180 centimeters), and
- "outside the talking zone" (farther than 6 feet or 180 centimeters).

---

* Edward T. Hall, *The Hidden Dimension* (Garden City, NY: Doubleday, 1966).

Classroom Adaptations

The following visual cues can be used to help students recognize personal space in the classroom.

Use colored plastic tape or masking tape to section off each student's area of a table.

- Place tape on the floor around each student's desk or area.
- Place tape or footprints on the floor to mark where each student should stand when waiting in line.
- On the playground or in the gym, use tape, chalk, or paint to denote where students should stand to wait their turns to play a game or shoot baskets.
- When students are seated on the floor, have them sit on a carpet square or use tape to mark where they are to sit.

Personal Space

Personal Space Role Plays

Have students or staff members act out the "What's Personal Space? Role Plays" provided in Appendix 5-1.

Follow up each skit with a short discussion, using the following or similar questions:

- What did the speaker do wrong?
- How did the listener feel?
- How could you tell the listener felt that way?
  - Write students' responses on the board or chart paper. Include observations about leaning, turning, moving or looking away, tense and closed body posture, worried or angry facial expressions.

Have the actors repeat each skit, having students direct the "close talker" on where to stand and sit.

Model and Practice

Explain the following:

- People have invisible bubbles around them. When someone comes into your "personal bubble," that makes you feel uncomfortable. It could be compared to a stranger walking into the backyard of your home without permission.
- When talking with others, you should usually stand in the "talking zone." This is outside of the personal bubble and approximately two to six feet (60 centimeters to 1.8 meters) away from the other person. (Exceptions to the rule will be discussed later.)

Pair up students and have them face each other. Tell students to repeatedly step towards each other until they are very close to each other (18 inches or 45 centimeters or less). Discuss the following.

- How does it make you feel, having someone standing so close?

- Can you tell how your partner is feeling from the way he is standing or the look on his face?
- It's important not to go into others' personal space unless it's necessary because...
    - ○ Most people feel uncomfortable when other people get too close.
    - ○ When someone gets too close, others may think that person is being a bully or that there is something "wrong" with him.

Personal Space Bubbles

Hand out copies of the "Personal Space" illustration from Appendix 5-2, or place a copy on an overhead projector. Explain that since personal space bubbles are invisible, it's hard to know where they are. Ask students to tell what they observe about personal space bubbles from the illustration.

- They extend about 2 feet (60 centimeters) in front and back, or about one arm's length.
- They are smaller to your sides, usually about 12 to 18 inches (30 to 45 centimeters).

Demonstrate how big personal space bubbles are by having students take turns standing with one arm extended in front while another student approaches.

Measuring Personal Space

Explain that the size of personal space bubbles varies with different people. It's smaller with people we know and like. Students capable of measuring distances using a yardstick or meter stick can find their own comfort zone by doing the following.

- Divide students into groups of three or more and give each group a yardstick or meter stick for measuring.
- Have two individuals within each group stand a comfortable distance from each other and carry on a conversation, while a third person measures from one person's toes to the other person's toes and writes the distance measured.
- Still carrying on a conversation, have the two individuals move farther and farther apart until it feels uncomfortable because they are too far apart. Measure and write down that distance.
- Switch roles and repeat.

More advanced students could calculate the average comfort zone for all students.

Figuring Out What It Means

On the board or a large sheet of paper, draw the "Too Close—What Does It Mean?" chart similar to the one in Appendix 5-3. Discuss why someone would enter another's personal space and write the reasons under "Possible reasons" on the chart. Students could write the responses onto individual copies. (See example on next page.)

Too Close—What Does It Mean?	
Possible reasons	What to look for
<ul><li>wants to be friendly</li><li>angry or wants to bully</li><li>it's crowded</li><li>doesn't know that he's too close</li><li>needs to be close—doctor exam, telling secret</li></ul>	<ul><li>friendly or unfriendly body pointing?</li><li>relaxed or tense posture?</li><li>type of facial expression?</li><li>what's going on? is there a reason the person might be mad?</li></ul>

Next, ask students: if someone gets too close to you, how can you tell what the reason is? What do you need to look at or consider? Write their responses under "What to look for."

Using Video Clips

Play the following video clips with the sound off, asking students to watch the characters' personal space and tell what they are communicating. Watch again with the sound on.

- *My Summer Story*—Scene #6, towards the end at 00:40:40.
- *Cool Runnings*
  - Chapter #5, from 00:16:10—00:16:55. Why does Irv move into the other man's personal space? (To intimidate, show that he would not change his mind.)
  - Chapter 6, from 00:21:50—00:22:40. Why did the man invade the other's personal space? (To intimidate or scare him.) What else did the man do to show that he was trying to intimidate or scare the man? (Poke him in the chest with his finger.)

Homework Assignment

Give students an assignment of looking for examples in real life of one person approaching another person, making eye contact, and entering the person's talking zone.

This could be done on the playground, at lunch, at home, in the community, or even on TV. Ask the students to observe the body language, decide on the reason for the invasion, and write a short description of what they observed or be ready to tell about it in class.

Adjusting to Space Invaders

Demonstrate with another staff person or a student who has been cued what to do. Begin by allowing the student to stand a comfortable distance from you while you carry on a conversation. Then move closer to the student, having the student shift his or her position to maintain appropriate personal space. Continue to move towards the person, as the person moves back to adjust. Discuss what people can do to protect their personal space.

- Pair up students to role-play.
- Designate which student will be the space invader and which one will do the adjusting.
- Instruct students to carry on a conversation while they are invading and adjusting. Have students do this for 20 to 30 seconds. It's often helpful to give students a topic to talk about, such as what type of music they like or what they watch on TV.
- Have students switch roles and repeat.
- Discuss reactions and observations.

Exceptions to the Rule

On the board or a large sheet of paper, draw the "Inside a Personal Space Bubble" chart from Appendix 5-4. Ask the following questions, writing the responses on the chart as shown below. Students could write the responses on individual blank charts.

- Is it OK for some people to enter your personal space bubble?
- Which people can enter your bubble?
- What happens inside personal space bubbles?

Inside a Personal Space Bubble	
Who	What happens
<ul><li>family</li><li>close friends</li><li>doctors, nurse, dentists, therapists</li><li>boyfriend or girlfriend</li><li>teammates</li><li>shoe salesman</li></ul>	<ul><li>talk quietly</li><li>talk about private things</li><li>tell secrets</li><li>doctor & dentist exams</li><li>show affection, hug, kiss</li></ul>

Asking Permission

Sometimes it's necessary to go into another's personal space, even though you don't know the person that well. Provide an example, such as dropping your pencil and having it land under another student's desk. Ask students the following:

- What are some other examples of times you need to go into another person's personal space?
- What should you do, if you need to enter another person's personal space?
  - Ask permission or say "excuse me."
  - If you need to get someone's attention and he doesn't hear you, lightly touch him on the shoulder.

Write the following examples on the board or use examples students gave. Use the first example to demonstrate for the students how you would enter someone's personal space. Pair up students and have them take turns entering each other's personal space. Ask for volunteers to demonstrate in front of the class.

- Your pencil is under another student's chair.
- Two people are standing talking in a doorway that you need to enter.
- You need to tell another student that his/her zipper is unzipped.
- You need to step over someone's feet to get to your seat at the movies.
- Someone is standing in front of your locker or cubby and you need to get into it.
- You dropped some money at the store and it is next to someone's feet.
- Someone is sitting on your coat.

Among Strangers

Line up a number of chairs side by side and tell students to pretend that they are at a doctor's office (or other familiar setting) and they need to wait to see the doctor. Everyone in the waiting room is a stranger. Ask students to enter and take a seat one at a time.

Ask students to explain why they chose the seat they chose. Explain that there is an unwritten rule that strangers do not sit next to each other, unless no other seat is available. People feel uncomfortable when a stranger sits or stands close to them.

Take Your Places

Create a pretend elevator by designating an area of the floor (approximately 5 feet by 6 feet or 1.5 by 2 meters) using masking tape or furniture. Indicate where the door and buttons are. Ask students to keep in mind personal space as they get on the elevator, push the button for their floor (or ask someone to push it), stand, and exit the elevator. Discuss the unwritten rules for riding an elevator—stand with your back against the wall until it gets crowded, then face the front of the elevator, look to the front, don't look at people, etc. Practice in a real elevator, if one is available.

Other scenarios that you can use to help students learn the rules for personal space in crowded public settings:

- Set up a pretend theater by placing empty chairs in rows. Have students line up to buy their tickets and then enter the theater and choose a seat.
- Set up a pretend bus with chairs and have students enact riding on a crowded bus with strangers.
- Discuss where to sit in a public or school locker room.
- For groups of boys, discuss how to choose which urinal to use in a restroom (whichever unused one is farthest away from others that are being used).

Homework Assignment

Give students an assignment to look at how people act when in a situation with strangers, such as at a movie theater, doctor or dentist office, waiting in line, on an elevator, etc. Have students report on what they observed.

In Crowded Situations

Distribute copies of "In a Crowd" from Appendix 5-5. Ask students to check what these people are doing.

Tell students that when people are in a crowded situation with strangers, they generally exhibit the following behaviors:
- They stand or sit quite still.
- Their faces have a blank expression.
- They do not look at each other. They will stare off into space or look down.

Have students pretend to be on a crowded bus or in a crowded elevator with strangers.

Marking Your Territory

Introduce this topic by taking a personal item, such as your sweater or book, and placing it on a student's desk or where he usually sits. Or move an item a student has used to indicate where he is going to sit, such as moving his notebook from the desk he has chosen. Discuss the student's reaction and why he feels invaded.

Ask students to think of examples of how people mark their territory, such as placing a coat or sweater on a chair, placing a towel on a beach chair, putting books on a table at the library, etc.

Point out that it's important that others recognize that an object is a marker and not just some litter that got left behind. Ask what types of objects are found on tables and chairs that are usually just trash, such as old newspapers, magazines, or empty and disposable cups.

Give students a homework assignment to write a description, tell about, or draw a picture of someone marking his or her territory.

Touching

When Is Touching OK?

Give students copies of the "Different Kinds of Touching Role Plays" from Appendix 5-6 and have pairs of students act out each role play. (Or act out the role plays yourself with a student volunteer or another staff person.)

Discuss whether the touching in the role play was appropriate or not. If not, why not?

Types of Touching

Distribute copies of the "OK Types of Touch" chart, Appendix 5-7 and draw a similar chart on the board. Discuss and list appropriate types of touching, including the items in the chart below. (More information on shaking hands is included in the unit on Gestures and Greetings.)

OK Types of Touch			
Type	With Whom	Why	How
• touch or tap • pat • handshake • affectionate touching (holding hands, hugging, kissing, snuggling)	• anyone • family & friends • anyone • family: close friend, boyfriend, girlfriend, husband, wife (only when they like it)	• get attention • say, "good job"; say, "it's OK" • meet someone new • show affection	• lightly on shoulder • lightly on shoulder or back • shake right hand • gently

Create a "Not OK Types of Touch" chart from Appendix 5-8. Ask students to list inappropriate and accidental touching and what to do, as in the chart below. Copy answers onto individual charts, if desired.

Not OK Types of Touch		
Types	What to Do *if you do it*	What to Do *if done to you*
• Touches that hurt or bully (hit, push, slap, pinch, poke)	• stop it	• report it
• Touching off-limit parts of body	• stop it	• report it
• Touching someone who does not want to be touched	• stop it	• report it
• Touching someone's hair, clothes, or belongings	• stop it	• say, "Don't"
• Accidental touch (bump, stepping on someone's foot)	• Say, "Sorry" or "Excuse me"	• don't get mad

Where to Touch

Distribute copies of the "Where to Touch" worksheet, Appendix 5-9. Describe age-appropriate situations (see examples below) and have students mark on the corresponding silhouette where the touching should or should not occur (see example on page 48).

1. You need to walk past a man in a crowded room. His back is turned to you and he didn't hear you when you said, "excuse me." Mark where you would touch him.
2. Your friend just won first prize. Where could you touch him to congratulate him?
3. Mark the parts of the body that a parent, close family member, or close friend can touch that other people generally shouldn't touch.
4. You've just been introduced to someone. What part of his or her body can you touch?
5. Mark the parts of the body that should not be touched except in special situations, such as if someone has an appointment with a doctor or nurse or if two people are married or lovers.
6. The teacher is talking and doesn't see you. Where can you touch her to get her attention?
7. Show where you could touch your good friend to show that you really like him or her.

Additional Learning Activities

The Growing Circle

Have two students go to the center of an open area and carry on a friendly conversation. Next, have another student join the twosome. Ask students to note how positions needed to be shifted. Continue adding one student at a time, noting how positions shift to accommodate body orientation and personal space.

Repeat the activity using chairs. Start with an open area with chairs available outside of the area. Have two students each take a chair to the center of the area and place their chairs so that they will be able to talk together.

Next, have another student (with a chair) join the twosome. Note how positions need to be shifted to accommodate body orientation and personal space. Continue adding one student (with a chair) at a time.

Stop Action

Play short segments of DVDs with the sound turned off. Hit pause and have students point out the different amount of personal space between characters.

The *Seinfeld: Season 5* DVD has a great example of a "close-talker" in the 18th episode, entitled "The Raincoat—Part 1." This DVD is often available at public libraries or video rental stores.

Where to Touch

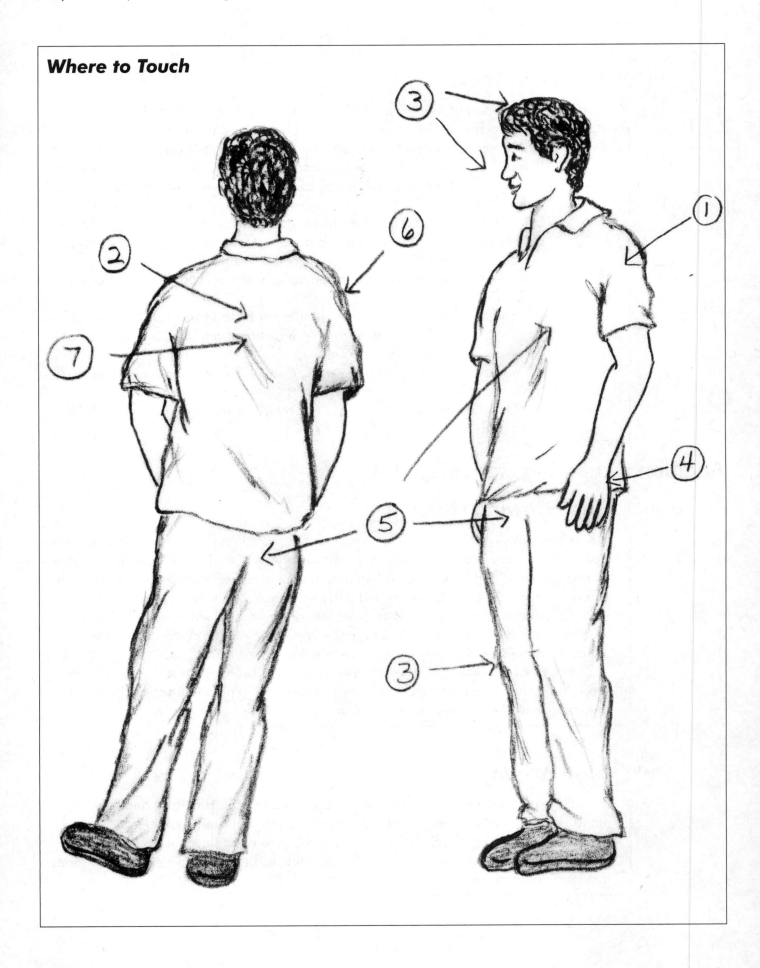

Treasure Hunt

Have students collect pictures of couples and groups of people from old magazines and picture books. Have students share their pictures with the class, telling what they think is happening in the pictures (the relationship between the people, how they are feeling, what they are probably thinking or saying).

 ## Candid Camera

Take photos of students as they go through their daily activities. At a later time, look over the photos and point out examples of personal space. Ask the students to tell you whether people are too close to one another.

 ## Posed Pictures

Take photos of students modeling appropriate and inappropriate personal space. Label and display the pictures.

 ## Create a Scene

Make copies of the "Create a Scene" scenarios from Appendix 5-10 and distribute them to students. Have students cut apart the scenarios and glue them on sheets of paper (one scenario per paper). Next, have students draw or cut out figures from old catalogs or magazines and place them on the pages to depict each scene. Paper dolls could also be used. (See example.)

Three friends are standing and talking to each other.

Sunday Funnies

Make copies of cartoons or comic strips. Place them on the overhead and have students point out personal space between characters. See the list of comic strips on page 24.

Too Close, Too Far, Just Right Role Plays

Copy and distribute the role plays from Appendix 5-11. Pair up students and have them perform the role plays standing too close, then too far away, then within the talking zone. Discuss differences in how it feels when conversation partners are too close or too far away.

Read, Pause, and Pose

Read aloud a story that involves a variety of actions and emotions. Pause at points in the story and ask students to demonstrate the characters' postures, body orientation, eye gaze, and personal space. When first using this activity, use picture books and show students the pictures, then have students model the postures. Once students become adept at this, have them display the postures before showing them the pictures in the book.

Read, Pause, and Draw

Follow the directions for "Read, Pause, and Pose," except instead of having students take poses, have students draw pictures of the characters as they would appear in the story.

Personal Space Reminder Story

A reminder story about personal space is provided in Appendix 5-12. Other additional stories could be written to address specific problems or situations.

Activity Pages

Make copies of appendices 5-13, 5-14, 5-15, 5-16, and 5-17:
- "Personal Space"
- "Where Would You Sit?"
- "Touching"
- "Read the Body Language"
- "Read the Body Language—Part 2"

Have the students complete them in groups or individually.

End of Unit Quiz

Have students take the Unit Quiz—Personal Space and Touching in Appendix 5-18.

Chapter 6

Gestures

Introduction

While most of us pay little attention to the gestures we use, we consciously or unconsciously ascribe a great deal of meaning to the gestures we see. Gestures grab the attention of the listener and communicate considerable information, whether used with or without accompanying verbal language. Using gestures with words usually delivers a much stronger message than words alone. And if words and gestures do not match—for example, shaking the head no while saying, "I believe you"—the listener is more likely to believe the nonverbal message.*

While there are far too many gestures to try to teach all of them, it is important to help students recognize the most commonly used, age appropriate gestures. Most gestures fall into one of the following categories:

1. greetings,
2. expressions of approval or disapproval, and
3. gestures that provide information.

This unit covers the most common gestures, but which gestures are used by different groups and in different situations is always changing. Therefore, it can be helpful to take note of the commonly used gestures in the child's environments and include them, using similar strategies and activities.

 Guess What It Means

Introduce gestures by demonstrating the following and see if students can guess what they mean:

- nod for "yes"
- shake head "no"
- waving
- finger to lips
- okay sign
- hand out, palm forward (stop)
- pointing

---

* Stephen Nowicki and Marshall Duke, *Helping the Child Who Doesn't Fit In* (Atlanta, GA: Peachtree Publishers), 1992, p. 7.

- thumbs up
- hand out, palm up (give me)
- shrugging (I don't know)
- finger wiggle (come here)
- finger wag (shame on you)

Explain that the above actions are called gestures, which are body movements that express a feeling or an idea. Explain that gestures can be used alone or with words by acting out the following:

Have another adult or student ask you several simple "yes" or "no" questions. (Questions could be written out ahead of time.) Answer the questions by using a gesture (a head nod or headshake) in addition to answering "yes" or "no." Have the other person ask several more "yes" or "no" questions, and this time answer with a head nod or shake, but no verbal response. Ask students if they understood what your answer was.

Next, have the adult or student ask another "yes" or "no" question, and this time verbally answer "yes" while shaking your head "no." (This is actually rather hard to do.) Try the reverse as well--nodding "yes" while saying, "no." Ask students whether they believe what you're saying and why your response is confusing.

Part 1: Greeting Gestures

The most commonly used gestures are greetings. Gestures included in this unit are the eyebrow flash, wave, hug, handshake, and fist bump. Students may have other types of greetings that they like to use, such as a "hang loose" gesture. These gestures can be included using activities similar to the ones listed below.

Saying Hello

 ### Saying Hello and Saying Good-bye—When and How

The charts in Appendix 6-1 and 6-2 provide an aid for discussing the basic rules for saying hello and good-bye, which students need to understand before discussing the gestures that accompany these greetings.

It may be helpful to determine what students already know by enlarging the charts and covering each statement with a strip of paper; e.g., "When you see someone you know for the 1st time each day." (See example at right.) Have students try to guess what is written under the strips of paper. Then uncover the steps and see how many steps they were able to name.

You may want to point out that when people see each other frequently throughout the day, such as at school or in a classroom, they generally greet each other when

Saying Hello
When to say hello
• When you see someone you know for the 1st time each day
• To start a conversation
How to say hello

they see each other for the first time that day. After that, they may smile or nod, but usually don't greet each other again until they say good-bye.

Saying Hello Chart—Different Ways to Say Hello and Good-bye

It's important for students to understand that different greetings are used with different people. You don't greet the principal the same way you greet your best friend. As a group, have the students fill out both the "Hello" and "Good-bye" charts, Appendix 6-1 and 6-2, with appropriate greetings for each group.

Different Ways to Say Hello		
Adults	Kids	Strangers
• Hello • Hello, Mr. Roberts • Good morning • Good morning, Mrs. Baker	• Hi! • Hi, Dylan • How's it going? • Hey, guys! • What's happening? • Hey man! • Hey, what's up?	• Hello • Hi. How are you? • Good morning

Role Plays

Have students role-play greeting each other in the following situations. Add other situations that students frequently encounter.
- Coming into the classroom for the first time that day
- Starting a conversation
- Passing others in the hall
- Going different ways after playing together
- Going back to class after working with a special teacher
- Parent drops you off at school

Eyebrow Flash

Throughout the world, the eyebrow flash is used to acknowledge and greet people we know. It involves a rapid raising and lowering of the eyebrows one time. It may accompany a verbal greeting, or be used as a nonverbal greeting.

Model and Practice

Ask students to watch your face carefully as a student or staff person walks toward you. As the person begins to get close, look at the person, smile, and flash your eyebrows, but don't greet the person in any other way. Ask students what they observed and why it can be important to greet others in this way. (It lets the person know that you are aware she's there, that you recognize her, and that you are glad to see her.)

Have students practice the eyebrow flash while looking at themselves in mirrors.

Pair up students and have them approach each other, giving an eyebrow flash and making eye contact.

 ## Video Clips

Play the following video clips and ask students to watch for the eyebrow flash and tell what is being communicated.

- *The Sandlot*—beginning of scene #2, at 00:03:25.
- *Akeelah and the Bee*—towards the beginning of scene #6, Javier gives an eyebrow flash after saying, "Lucky 13."
- *A Christmas Story*—scene 17, the teacher eyebrow flashes after Ralph winks, acknowledging the interaction.
- *How to Eat Fried Worms*—Scene #4, 00:13:29–00:13:34. The boy eyebrow flashes to acknowledge that the paper airplane was from him.
- *Freaks and Geeks*—Episode #117, Chapter 4, from 00:34:38–00:34:46. Nick eyebrow flashes Lindsay when she turns to say good-bye.
- *Freaks and Geeks*—Episode #108, Chapter 1, from 00:10:50–00:10:55. Nick eyebrow flashes Lindsay when she looks out the window at him.

 ## Pass the Flash

Stand in a line or circle. The teacher begins by getting the attention of the student next to him and gives an eyebrow flash. That student turns to the student next to him and gives an eyebrow flash. Continue around the circle or to the end of the line.

 ## Flash Tag

Stand or sit in a circle. One person begins by randomly choosing another person in the circle to eyebrow flash. That person returns the flash, then selects another person to eyebrow flash. Continue until everyone has had a turn.

 ## Greeting Gestures Chart

On the board or a large sheet of paper, draw the "Gestures ~ Greetings" chart from Appendix 6-3. Discuss and fill in the eyebrow flash section of the chart. Students could write the responses onto individual copies. (See example below.) Include the following information:

- Who uses it?—people who know each other
- When & where?—when you first see someone you know

Gestures ~ Greetings

Type	Who uses it	When & where	What it means
eyebrow flash	people who know each other	when you first see someone you know	I see you. I know you.
wave			
hug			

- What it means?—I see you or I recognize you

To add additional greetings, there is a blank space on the second page of the "Greetings ~ Gestures" chart, Appendix 6-4, as well as an additional blank chart in Appendix 6-5.

Art and Animation

Use the drawings and directions in Appendix 6-6 to create an animation flipbook of an eyebrow flash. More advanced students could create flipbooks using their own drawings.

Wave

The wave is a common worldwide gesture to say hello or good-bye or to get someone's attention from a distance. When used from a distance to gain attention, the arm is extended so the hand is held over the head. This is used to acknowledge someone, to indicate a desire to speak with the person, to seek help, or in classroom situations to signal that you want to speak. When giving a friendly wave, such as when passing a friend in the hall, the hand is held up so it is at approximately shoulder or head level.

Model and Practice

Ask students to name four different reasons people wave at each other. (See list below.) If students need help, act out short scenarios demonstrating how the wave is used.
- To say hello
- To say good-bye
- To get someone's attention (from a distance)

- To let the teacher know you want to say something
- To tell someone to stop

Have students act out the following or similar role plays, using waving.
- Passing a friend in the hall
- Seeing a friend at recess or at break
- Saying good-bye to a friend after a break or recess
- Seeing a friend in the lunchroom
- Trying to get a friend's attention from across the gym
- Saying good-bye to a parent dropping you off at school

Wave Tag

Stand or sit in a circle. One person begins by randomly choosing another person in the circle to wave at. That person returns the wave, then selects another person and waves to him or her. Continue until everyone has had a turn.

Flash or Wave Tag

Repeat the above activity, having the person who is "it" *either* wave to or eyebrow flash another person in the circle. The receiver then either waves to or eyebrow flashes someone else.

Telling Someone to Stop

Quickly waving the hand sideways and shaking the head or saying "no," indicate that you want someone to stop doing or saying something. Model and have students practice this gesture in both emergency and more subtle situations.
- Show how this gesture would be used as a warning to prevent someone from stepping out into traffic.
- Then show how it would be used to tell someone not to talk about a sensitive topic.

Greeting Gestures Chart

Fill in the wave section on the "Gesture ~ Greetings" chart, Appendix 6-3.
- Who uses it?—wave at people you know
- When and where?—saying hello or good-bye, anywhere
- What does it mean?—hello, good-bye, I have something to say, I need help, stop

Guess What It Means Game

Use the following activity to demonstrate the different kinds of waves and how waves look different depending on the emotional content of the situation.

Copy or write out the following scenarios and cut into strips. Have students draw a scenario to act out. Write the scenarios on the board and have students guess which scenario is being acted out. If this is too difficult, give students two scenarios to choose between.

You see a friend way across the room. You wave so he will see you.
You see someone you know in the hall and wave to her.
Someone is hurt and you are waving at the teacher to get help.
You are waving good-bye to a good friend who is moving away.
You are gesturing to someone to tell him that he picked up your backpack instead of his own.
Someone you don't like waved at you. You wave back.
You see a friend who you haven't seen in a long time. You wave so he will see you.

Worksheet

Have the students complete the "Waving - What Does It Mean?" worksheet, Appendix 6-7 and 6-8.

Hugging

In recent years, it has become much more common for teenagers and young adults to hug their friends as a way of greeting each other. But hugging is different from other greetings in that virtually everyone is expected to wave, look at others, nod, say hello, and shake hands. However, some people do not like to be hugged, so initiating a hug requires more social awareness. It's best to teach students to wait for the other person to initiate the hug unless they are greeting family or very close friends.

Model and Practice

Act out a short scenario with a student or staff person, approaching each other, saying hello, and giving each other a hug. Ask students what they saw and how they feel about hugging. Explain that with most people it's better to use a sideways hug, or, if facing each other, to leave some space between your body and the other person's. Model these types of hugs. Ask for student volunteers to demonstrate hugging.

Video Clips

Play the following video clips and ask students to watch for characters hugging each other. Ask them whether they think the hugging is mutual and appropriate and what it communicates.

- *Freaks and Geeks,* Episode #108, Chapter 2, from 00:15:15–00:15:30, Cindy hugs Sam to congratulate him.
- *Freaks and Geeks,* Episode #113, Chapter 1, from 00:10:20–00:10:40— Lindsay hugs her friend to comfort her.
- *Freaks and Geeks,* Episode #110, Chapter 1, from 00:07:08–00:07:12— An example of hugging from the side.
- *Freaks and Geeks,* Episode #100, Chapter 1, at 00:06:20—An example of an inappropriate hug.

Greeting Gestures Chart

Fill in the hugging section on the "Gestures ~ Greetings" chart, Appendix 6-3.

- Who uses it?—family and close friends
- When & where?—when saying hello or good-bye, to comfort someone, to show affection
- What does it mean?—"Good to see you," "I care about you," "I like you."

Worksheet: Hugging—What Does It Mean?

Distribute the "Hugging - What Does It Mean?" worksheet (Appendix 6-9). Since how things are said is at least as important as what is said, it may be helpful to read the statements to the students, using a really sad voice to read the first statement, a happy voice for the second, and a rather casual voice for the third statement.

Hugging Quiz

Distribute the Hugging Quiz from Appendix 6-10.

Shaking Hands

Model and Practice

Before discussing *when* people shake hands, it's good to know how to do it right. Begin by going around the room and extending your hand and shaking hands with each student.

Next, use the chart in Appendix 6-11 to go over the steps for how to shake hands. Model each step with a student or another staff person. Pair up students and have them practice.

The simplest rule for students to learn is to recognize when someone is initiating a handshake and then reciprocate by shaking the person's hand.

Video Clips

- *The Sandlot*—Scene #25 at 00:33:08, to show agreement to a deal or plan.
- *How to Eat Fried Worms*—Scene #14, 00:55:12–00:55:22, meeting someone new.
- *Freaks and Geeks*—Episode #107, Chapter 3, from 00:24:15–00:24:19
- *Freaks and Geeks*—Episode #108, Chapter 4, from 00:32:10–00:32:26, an usually long handshake

Gestures ~ Greetings Chart

Fill in the handshake section on the "Gestures ~ Greetings" chart, Appendix 6-4.
- Who uses it?—strangers and people who know each other
- When & where?—when meeting someone new, when someone won or did something really good, to show agreement
- What does it mean?—"I'm glad to meet you," "Congratulations!" "I agree"

Handshake Role Plays

Model each of the following role plays. Then group students and have them act out each scenario, taking turns playing different roles.
- Two people introduce themselves to each other.
- One person introduces the other two people to each other.
- One person congratulates another for winning a game or prize.
- Several people come to an agreement, such as each agreeing to play fair.

Handshake Quiz

Copy and distribute the Handshake Quiz, Appendix 6-12.

Fist Bumps

A number of variations of a fist bump are sometimes used as informal greetings, both in saying hello and good-bye. They are also used to show agreement or approval or to wish someone good luck.

Model and Practice

Ask students what kinds of informal hand greetings they have observed, and have them demonstrate what they have seen.

Demonstrate the fist bump with a student or adult, gently touching the knuckles together, as seen in the chart on activity page 6-4. Have students practice the fist bump with each other.

Pass the Bump

Repeat the "Pass the Flash" activity on page 56, using a fist bump in place of the eyebrow flash.

Video Clips

- *Akeelah and the Bee*—Scene #6, from 00:24:00–00:24:20.
- *Freaks and Geeks*—Episode #107, Chapter 1, from 00:00:20–00:00:25.

Greetings - Gestures Chart

Fill in the fist bump section on the "Gestures ~ Greetings" chart, Appendix 6-4.
- Who uses it?—friends, family
- When & where?—saying hello or good-bye, to show agreement, when someone won or did something good
- What it means?—hello, good-bye, I agree, congratulations, good luck

Worksheet - Bump or No Bump?

Complete the "Bump or No Bump?" worksheet from Appendix 6-13, discussing when a fist bump is appropriate. Tell the students that when in doubt, it's best not to initiate a fist bump.

Additional Learning Activities

Posed Pictures

Take photos of students modeling different greetings—waving, doing an eyebrow flash, shaking hands, hugging, fist bumping. Discuss and label the greetings seen in the photos. More advanced students could create scenarios in which the greetings occurred.

Greetings Tag

Stand or sit in a circle. Select someone to be "it." That person "tags" another person in the circle by greeting that person in some way. The student could use an eyebrow flash or a wave, or she could go up to the person and shake her hand, give a fist bump, or other type of greeting. That person then tags someone else with a greeting.

Worksheet: Which Greeting?

Have students answer the multiple-choice questions on the "Which Greeting?" worksheet, Appendix 6-14, either individually or as a group.

Worksheets: Draw the Picture

Copy the two "Draw the Picture" worksheets from Appendix 6-15 and 6-16 and have students draw pictures showing each greeting.

Homework Assignment

Have students observe others at school, home, or in the community and report back about greeting gestures they observed. Students could keep a tally of the number of waves, hugs, fist bumps, etc. they observed. Students who are able could write a sentence telling what was happening when the greeting occurred.

Part 2: Approval & Disapproval Gestures

Probably the second most common gestures after greetings are those used to express approval and disapproval. This curriculum provides activities for ten of the most common ones, including head nods and shakes, thumbs up and down, cheering, high five, OK sign, finger wag, rolling the eyes, and the nose wrinkle. Additional gestures can be taught using similar types of activities.

Head Nodding and Shaking

To clarify the use of terms, in this curriculum the word "nod" refers to moving the head up and down to indicate approval or agreement (yes) and "shake" refers to moving the head side to side to indicate disapproval or disagreement (no).

Model and Practice—Headshake and Nod

Write a short list of items that you like and don't like, all mixed together. These could be foods, types of music, TV shows, or anything. Ask students to watch you while you read the list or have someone else read it. After each item is read, pause and either nod or shake your head. You might want to exaggerate your head movements, indicating likes and dislikes, but try to keep your facial expressions neutral.

After students have observed your reaction to a few items, continue with the list, pausing after you nod or shake your head, and ask the students whether they think you like that item. Discuss how head movements are used to express likes and dislikes, often without a person saying anything.

Pair up students and provide them with lists of items. Students take turns saying the item while the other indicates likes and dislikes with a nod or headshake. For students who do not read well, use pictures of items instead.

Model and Practice—Headshake to Express Disbelief

Repeat the activity above, but this time have a student or staff person read a set of statements, some obviously true and some obviously false, such as "It snows in the summer." Nod or shake your head to indicate whether you believe or don't believe the statement.

Discuss how a nod can indicate that you believe or know something to be true, and how a headshake can show that you do not believe what is being said.

Repeat the activity above, pairing up students and having them take turns reading and reacting to the statements.

Video Clips

- *Freaks and Geeks*—Episode #108, Chapter 2, from 00:19:33–00:16:38. What is Lindsay communicating by shaking her head? (That she does not want to talk to the boy who is on the phone.)
- *Akeelah and the Bee*—Scene #22, from 01:38:45–01:39:32. Dr. Laramie shakes his head after Dylan spells the word wrong. What is he expressing? (Disbelief. He was sure Dylan knew how to spell the word.)
- *The Sandlot*—Scene #7, from 00:18:30–00:19:40. Reaction when Scotty does not catch the ball and hands it to the pitcher.
- *Cool Runnings*—Chapters #8 & 9, 00:34:03–00:34:30 and 00:41:00–00:41:30. Why is Irv shaking his head "no" in both video clips? (To show disbelief.)

Approval/Disapproval Gesture Charts

On the board or a large sheet of paper, draw the "Gestures ~ Approval" and the "Gestures ~ Disapproval" charts from Appendix 6-17 and 6-18. Discuss and fill in the head nod and headshake sections on the charts. Include the information below. Students could write the responses onto individual copies of charts. Blank charts are provided in Appendix 6-19 and 6-20, if you choose to add other gestures.

Head Nod:
When & where?
- When the other person or persons are looking at you
- When you agree or like what was said or done

What does it mean?
- "Yes"
- "I like that"
- "I agree"

Head Shake:
When & where?
- When other person or persons are looking at you
- When you don't agree or don't like what was said or done
- When you find something hard to believe

What does it mean?
- "No"
- "I don't like that"
- "I think you are wrong"
- "I won't do it"
- "I didn't do it"
- "I can't believe it!"

Rapid Head Nods

This gesture requires more awareness and may be too subtle for some students, and therefore is not included on the "Approval Gestures" chart. It may be added to a blank "Approval Gesture" Chart for those students who are ready.

When someone nods his or her head quickly and repeatedly, it usually shows impatience. The person may be in a hurry to leave or wants to speak.

Model and Practice

Ask students to observe as you model the rapid nod, while a staff person or student talks to you. Discuss the following:
- What the gesture means
- Examples of when the gesture is used
- What the speaker should do when she sees the speaker nodding rapidly

Pair up students and have them take turns being the speaker and the listener. The listener should alternately practice patiently nodding in agreement and rapidly nodding. When the speaker sees the person nodding rapidly, she should pause to let the listener speak.

Thumbs Up & Thumbs Down

Model and Practice

These gestures indicate approval/disapproval or agreement/disagreement. Using thumbs up or down is generally not used to answer "yes" or "no" questions.

These gestures can be taught using the same activities used for head nods and shakes, skipping the activity involving "yes" and "no" questions.

Video Clips

- *The Sandlot*—thumbs up, Scenes #7 and #27, at 00:22:06 and 00:36:46.
- *Sandlot 2*—thumbs up, Scene #14, at 00:54:15.
- *High School Musical*—thumbs down, Scene #2, at 00:10:00.

Approval/Disapproval Gesture Charts

Complete the thumbs-up and thumbs-down section on the chart (Appendix 6-17 and 6-18), including the following information.

Thumbs-up:
When & where?
- When other person or persons are looking at you
- You agree with or like what was said or done

What does it mean?
- "I like that."
- "I agree."

Thumbs-down:
When & where?
- When other person or persons are looking at you
- When you don't agree with or don't like what was said or done

What does it mean?
- "I don't like that."
- "I think you are wrong,"

The "OK" Sign

The "OK" gesture is the best-known gesture in the United States, with 98 percent recognition, so students are likely to recognize it. To make this gesture, the thumb and index finger form an "O" with the rest of the fingers extended, as seen in the illustration on activity page 6-17.

Model and Practice

To review, ask students how they can show agreement without saying anything (head nod and thumbs-up). Ask if they can think of any other way to do this. If students don't come up with the "OK" gesture, demonstrate it and ask what it means. Discuss that it is used to indicate agreement ("I agree"; "It's OK for you to do that"; "OK, I understand."), as well as to show approval ("Good job!").

Ask students a number of simple yes or no questions, having each student respond nonverbally at the same time. Use questions that don't require much thought, such as "Do you like fried chicken?" Students should use the OK gesture if they agree or approve and shake their head if they disagree or disapprove.

"Getting the OK" Game

For younger children, a game can be played similar to "Mother May I?" A start and finish line is established, with the players standing on the start line and the leader standing alone on the finish line. The leader instructs one player at a time how she can move, such as, "Take two giant steps forward" (towards the finish line). But instead of the player asking, "Mother May I?" she asks, "Is it OK?" and the leader gives the OK gesture. As in "Mother May I?" if the player forgets to ask for permission, she needs to go back to the beginning and start over. The first player to reach the finish line wins.

For older students, you can play a game by telling them that during a certain period of time, every time you direct them to do something, they need to ask if it's OK. You will then respond by giving them the OK sign. For example, you might tell one student to go to the board. She would ask, "Is it OK?" and you would respond with the OK sign. Every time students remember to get the OK, the class earns one point. Every time the students forget to ask, one point is subtracted. When a set number of points have been earned, the class receives some type of reward.

Approval/Disapproval Gesture Charts

Complete the OK gesture section of the chart activity page 6-17, including the following information.

When & where?
- When another person or persons are looking at you
- You agree with or like what was said or done

What does it mean?
- "Yes"
- "I agree"
- "I like that"

The Finger Shake and Finger Poke

 ## Model and Practice

A finger shake is a gesture that communicates disapproval or anger. When the aggressor actually touches the other person with his finger, it becomes a finger poke. The purpose of both gestures is to intimidate the listener.

It's important to distinguish the finger shake from pointing the finger in the air to add emphasis to what one is saying.

Explain to students that you are going to say the same statement two times, but it will have a different meaning each time. Use one of the statements below, or make up your own. The first time you say it, point your index finger upward and shake it gently to emphasize what you are saying. Then repeat the statement using more of an angry tone of voice and wagging the finger in the listener's face in a scolding manner. Repeat the statement using the two gestures, stopping after each gesture to ask whether the speaker is angry with the listener. Say other statements, varying the type of gesture used and ask students to identify when you are angry. Statements:

- "It's important to take care of your pets."
- "The rule is that you need to share."
- "Pick up all the stuff on the floor."

Discuss how the two gestures look different:

Used for emphasis
- Finger points up
- Speaker does not lean toward listener
- Speaker's face does not look angry
- Speaker's voice does not sound angry

Used to scold
- Finger points at listener
- Speaker leans toward listener
- Speaker's face looks angry
- Speaker's voice sounds angry

Pair up students and have them practice acting out the scripts below, alternating who is doing the finger shake. The student chooses the type of finger shake (to emphasize or to scold) that seems appropriate for the situation. After practicing, have students act out the scripts for other students.

- "Look at this room! What a mess!"
- "I really like books about whales!"
- "Dogs make the best pets!"
- "I told you not to do that!"
- "You're in big trouble!"
- "Hey, I got a great idea!"
- "That is no way to act!"
- "Let's go to the comic book store this Saturday!"
- "I don't think that's the right answer."
- "You need to be quiet!"

Video Clips

Discuss how the finger can be slowly wagged sideways, to also indicate dislike, but in a gentler way, meaning, "Uh-uh, don't do that." Demonstrate or show the following movie clip.

- *Uncle Nino*—Scene #8 at 00:11:23. Uncle Nino finger wags his finger to say "no" to smoking.
- *Cheaper by the Dozen*—Scene #11 from 00:31:58–00:32:38.

 ## Disapproval Charts

Complete the finger shake section of the chart (Appendix 6-18), including the following information.

When & Where?
- When another person is looking at you
- When you are upset with another person

What it means?
- "I don't like what you did or said!"
- "Stop doing what you're doing"

The High Five

 ## Model and Practice

The high five is a celebratory gesture that originated in American team sports. The palms of two people are held up in the air and slapped together, as seen in the illustration on activity page 6-17.

Act out a short scenario with another staff member or student. Congratulate the person on some accomplishment (real or pretend), then give a high five. Ask students what the high five means.

Ask students if they can think of other times people give high fives. (When their team wins or they both get good news, such as that the class is going on a field trip.)

Next, ask students to watch carefully as you repeat the scenario, this time pausing as you raise your hand to initiate the high five. Ask students, "What am I doing?" (By raising your hand, palm out, you are telling the other person that you want to give a high five. The other person responds by mimicking your motion and making hand-to-hand contact.)

Pair up students, designating one student as student A and the other as student B. Describe scenarios to the students and have them give high fives. Use the scenarios below or make up your own.

- Student <u>A</u> congratulates student <u>B</u> for winning a drawing contest.
- <u>B</u> congratulates <u>A</u> for winning free movie tickets.
- <u>A</u> said that her all-time favorite movie is _____, and that is <u>B</u>'s favorite movie as well.
- <u>A</u> and <u>B</u> find out that their class gets to go see the animated dinosaur exhibit.

- *A* and *B* have won top prize for their science project.
- *A* and *B* were watching a game and their team just won.
- School is closing early because it's snowing.
- *B* said that _____ rules (is way cool, rocks, etc.), and *A* agrees.

When to Give a High Five

Repeat the activity above, but this time you are going to relate some situations where a high five would be appropriate, and some where it would not. Students should consider the situation and give a high five only when appropriate.

- Ethan and Anna are playing on the same team. Ethan scores a point by answering a question correctly.
- In the same game, Anna gives an incorrect answer to a question.
- Sam tells a joke that James really likes.
- Olivia and Maria are watching a game but are cheering for different teams. Olivia's team wins the game.
- Josh congratulates Emily for winning a $50 prize.
- Juan got an A+ on a test, but Michael got a D.
- Chris and Min both scored 100% on their tests.
- Sarah says the best video game in the world is _____, but Raj doesn't like that game.

Ask students how each student felt in each of these situations. When *both* parties are happy about what happened, a high five is appropriate.

Video Clips

- *The Sandlot*—Scene #27 at 01:36:00.
- *The Sandlot 2*—Scene #23, as player runs around the bases, beginning at 1:33:05.
- *How to Eat Fried Worms*—Scene #18, 01:15:08–01:15:14.
- *High School Musical*—Scene #9, at 00:12:57.

Approval Gesture Chart

Complete the high five section of the chart, Appendix 6-17, including the following information:

When & where?
- When other person or persons are close and looking at you
- Both people agree or like what just happened.

What does it mean?
- "Good job!"
- "I like that"
- "Congratulations!"

Clapping Hands

 ## Model and Practice

Ask students to think of a time when they have been at an assembly and someone was playing music. What did everyone do when the performance was finished? Discuss that people applaud to show that they like something, pointing out that people will applaud to be polite.

Have students respond nonverbally to their likes and dislikes by either clapping or giving a thumbs down. Use the list below or create items relevant to the students.

- The class is going on a fieldtrip.
- The class is going to have a popcorn party.
- The teacher gave lots of homework.
- You get to go see a movie.
- You need to clean your room.
- There's pizza for lunch.
- You're having a test at school.
- You got a new video game.
- You are having a party for your birthday.

 ## Approval Gesture Chart

Complete the clapping section on the chart (Appendix 6-17), including the following information:

When & where?
- When you agree with or like what was said or done.

What does it mean?
- "I agree"
- "I like that"
- "You did that really well!"

The Cheer

 ## Model and Practice

The cheering gesture refers to extending one or both arms into the air to express excitement. This gesture is often accompanied by verbal exclamations such as "Yay!" or "All right!" See the illustration on the chart, Appendix 6-17.

Show one of the following, or a similar clip from a movie showing people cheering. If a video clip is not available, describe a scene, such as watching a ball game, and demonstrate giving a cheer. Either show examples or model both a one-fisted and two-fisted cheer.

- Akeelah and the Bee
  - Scene #6—toward the end of scene #6, after Xaxier makes it into the final 10 contestants.

○ Throughout scenes #19 & 20.
- *My Summer Story*—Scene #4—Ralph talking with his dad at the dinner table.
- *The Sandlot*—Scene #27, at 01:36:00. The crowd and the players are cheering.
- *Sandlot 2*—Scene #23 at 1:33:05.
- *High School Musical*—Scene #12, from 01:30:00 to 01:31:05.

Ask students to describe and imitate what they saw the people in the video clip doing and why they were doing that. Cheering is somewhat different from many gestures since its purpose is less to communicate to others and more of a spontaneous expression of feelings.

When to Cheer

It is important to know when and where cheering is appropriate and to distinguish a cheer from an expression of anger or a threat (covered in the following section).

Describe the following or similar situations and have students respond by raising one or both hands when cheering is appropriate and shaking their heads when not appropriate.

- You just won a race you were running.
- You are watching a game and your team won.
- A really good player on the other team got hurt.
- You *finally* scored 100 on a video game you were playing.
- A friend says she likes your shirt.
- A friend you are playing against just messed up.
- The teacher just told your class that school is cancelled for the rest of the week.

Approval Gesture Chart

Complete the cheer section of the chart, Appendix 6-17, including the following information.

When & where?
- When you feel really excited about something
- You agree with or like what was said or done
- To congratulate yourself

What does it mean?
- "I really like that!"
- "I did it!"

The Fist

The fist is similar to a one-handed cheer, and can be misinterpreted if the child does not consider the context. A fist, which indicates a threat, is usually held in a different position and is coupled with an angry expression.

Model and Practice

Show one of the following video clips, or similar ones to indicate how the fist and finger poke are used as a threat.

- *My Summer Story*—Scene #4, the dad yelling at the neighbors makes a fist.
- *The Sandlot*—Scene #13, at 00:45:30 and 00:46:45, examples of fists. Play the scene with sound *off* to avoid colorful language.
- *Uncle Nino*—Scene #8 at 00:19:05, example of finger poke.
- *How to Eat Fried Worms*—Scene #5, 00:21:38–00:21:48, finger shake in face.
- *Freaks and Geeks*—Episode #114, Chapter 2, from 15:08–15:28, finger poke.

Ask students to describe what they saw in the video and what it meant. One of the clues in distinguishing a cheer from a threat is where the person holds his arm and fist. In a cheer, they are held to the *side* of the body, but with the fist they are held more in *front* of the body at the level of the neck or head, with the fist rotated so the back of the hand faces the other person. Have students face each other or look in a mirror and practice each position.

Discuss the importance of looking at the facial expression that accompanies the fist. Model a number of angry fists, randomly interspersed with one-handed cheers, and ask students to tell what each one is.

 What Is Happening?

Discuss that it's also important to consider what is going on and what the person is saying, to determine if it's a cheer or a fist. Read the following or similar quotes and ask students to tell whether you are cheering or threatening.

- "Hey! Alright!"
- "That's great!"
- "You'd better not try it!"
- "I dare you!"
- "We did it!"
- "You think you're so smart!"
- "*What* did you say?"
- "Yeah!"
- "I'm not kidding!"
- "We won!"

 Disapproval Gesture Chart

Complete the fist section of the chart, Appendix 6-18, including this information:

When & where?
- When facing another person
- To show anger
- To indicate that you may hit the other person

What does it mean?
- "You really make me mad!"
- "I feel like hitting you!"

The Nose Wrinkle

Model and Practice

The nose wrinkle involves scrunching up the nose and is often an unconscious reaction to a bad smell or unpleasant situation. Review how you indicated likes and dislikes by shaking or nodding your head (pages 63-65). Create a similar list of items you like and dislike. Ask students to watch your face while you or another person reads the list, pausing while you show approval by raising your eyebrows and slightly smiling or disapproving by wrinkling your nose. After each response have students tell what your face expressed.

Pair up students and provide them with lists of items. Students take turns saying the item while the other indicates likes and dislikes with a nod or nose wrinkle. Pictures of items can be used with students who do not read well.

Video Clips

- *A Christmas Story*—Scene 10, from minute 27:00 to 28:00. Watch for Ralph and his father wrinkling their noses in disgust as Randy eats like a little piggy.
- *My Summer Story*—Scene #4, Ralph wrinkles his nose as he smells what is cooking in the pot.
- *How to Eat Fried Worms*—Scene #1, 00:02:15–00:02:25. This movie is full of nose wrinkles to express disgust. This clip is the quickest to access.
- *Freaks and Geeks*—Episode #107, Chapter 2, from 00:12:30–00:13:15. Sam reacts to Gordon putting his pencil in his mouth and ear.

Disapproval Chart

Complete the nose wrinkle section of the chart, Appendix 6-18, including the following information:

When & where?
- To show dislike, disgust
- To indicate that you don't want to do something

What does it mean?
- "I don't like that."
- "That's disgusting!"
- "I don't want to do that."

The Eye Roll

Model and Practice

Ask a staff member or student to read the following or similar statements to you while the other students watch your face. After each statement, roll your eyes to one side and upward to express annoyance, frustration, or disbelief.

- "I know you think you work hard, but I actually work a lot harder than you do."
- "I can draw better than anyone in the school."
- "Did you make that? It's really ugly."

Ask students to describe what you did after each of the statements and what they think you were thinking when you rolled your eyes. Discuss how people are always moving their eyes and you have to watch how they move their eyes to recognize the eye roll. Have students watch as you move your eyes and indicate when they see the eye roll. Move your eyes in various ways, sometimes rolling them and sometimes not.

Explain that eye rolling is seen as disrespectful, particularly by adults, and discuss what can happen when a student rolls her eyes when speaking with a teacher, parent, coach, doctor, etc. Also, discuss what it likely means when an adult rolls her eyes when listening to a student.

Have students use mirrors to practice the eye roll. While the intent is not to encourage the use of the eye roll, the eye roll can be an unconscious gesture, so it's important for students to learn to recognize when they are actually using it.

Video Clips

- *Akeelah and the Bee*—Scene #5, at 00:18:25–00:18:35, during Akeelah's conversation with Dr. Larrabee, while saying, "Whatever!" And at 00:20:25 at very end of scene as her sister carries her crying baby.
- *My Summer Story*—Scene #3, from 00:14:30–00:15:50. The store clerk rolls his eyes when Ralph is deciding what to buy. A few seconds later, Ralph eye rolls when the clerk says they must take a red jaw breaker for every black one.
- *Sandlot 2*—Scene #3, at 00:10:10 (start at 00:09:42 to understand meaning)
- *Uncle Nino*—Scene #1, from 00:10:47–00:11:00. Joey (in the purple shirt) rolls head and eyes to show disapproval of what Bones (boy in black shirt) is saying.
- *Freaks and Geeks*, Episode #104, Chapter 4, from 00:38:44–00:39:00. This one is quick and not that easy to catch, as attention is on Mr. Kowchevski, the teacher who is standing. Watch the seated counselor after Mr. Kowchevski said he still believes the students had cheated.

Disapproval Chart

Complete the eye roll section of the chart, Appendix 6-18, including the following information:

When & where?
- When feeling frustrated
- When you don't like what someone said

What does it mean?
- "This is really hard!"
- "You are making me mad!"
- "I don't believe what you are saying."

Additional Activities

 ## Worksheets

Distribute copies of the three "What does it mean?" worksheets in Appendix 6-21, 6-22, and 6-23 for students to complete individually or as a group.

 ## Homework Assignment

Have the students observe interactions at home, at school, or in the community, watching for head shakes or nods, high fives, finger poking or shaking, nose wrinkles, cheers, etc. Students report back about approval and disapproval gestures they observed.

Part 3: Informational Gestures

This section includes common gestures that provide information and are often not accompanied with any verbal language. The first five informational gestures can be introduced by acting out the following pantomime with another staff person or student. Begin with person #1 and person #2 standing at least six feet apart. First act out the following sequence, pausing after each gesture to ask students what they think it means.

- Person #1: Look at person #2 and use finger to gesture, "come here."
- Person #1: As person #2 gets close, use raised hand to tell the person to stop.
- Person #1: Use finger to lips to gesture, "shhh!"
- Person #1: Point off into distance.
- Person #2: Shrug to indicate confusion.

Come Here

Explain and demonstrate that there are a variety of ways to gesture for someone to approach—using the index finger, using four fingers together, or using a whole arm movement. The person gesturing generally tries to make eye contact, so the observer knows that the gesture is meant for him or her. The exception is when someone is directing a crowd of people, such as an officer directing traffic. Sometimes people will gesture to someone who is already close to move even closer in order to whisper to her or tell her something they do not want others to hear.

Model and Practice

Pair up students and have them practice gesturing for each other to approach. Have students try gesturing from various distances, using larger, whole arm movements when farther apart, and smaller, finger gestures when closer. Also have them gesture as if they want to tell a secret and don't want everyone else to notice.

Informational Gesture Chart

A three-page chart for informational gestures is found in Appendix 6-24 and a blank chart is found in Appendix 6-25. Complete the "come here" gesture section of the chart, including the following information:

When & where?
- When you want the other person to come closer
- When you want to whisper something to the other person
- When the other person is looking at you

What does it mean?
- "Come closer."
- "Move this way."
- "I want to tell you a secret."

Stop

Model and Practice

Review the gesture for stop as demonstrated in the introductory activity, page 58. Then ask students to watch as you use the gesture in two different ways and ask them to tell you how the meanings differ. First use the stop gesture in a casual manner, as you might use it to indicate who should proceed in a line and who should wait. Next, use the gesture as it would be used in an emergency, with a sudden and exaggerated movement.

Discuss how the gesture can be used to stop someone from moving a certain direction and also to stop the person from doing or saying something. Demonstrate by having someone do something annoying, such as drumming on a table, and indicate for the person to stop, similar to the quick sideways wave described on page 57.

Pair up students and have them take turns gesturing to each other, alternating between gesturing "come here," and "stop."

Red Light, Green Light Game

Play a game similar to Red Light, Green Light. Have all except one player stand together at a designated starting line. One student stands at least 20 feet in front of the other students with eyes closed as she gestures for others to come here with her hand. She then makes the gesture for stop, and opens her eyes. If she spots a player moving, that player must go back to the start line. The first player to the finish line wins.

Video Clip

View one or more of the following video clips and have students observe use of the stop gesture.

- *Uncle Nino*—Scene #1 at 00:08:50, the father indicates he wants his son to stop talking while he is on the phone.
- *Akeelah and the Bee*—Scene #19 from 01:27:34–01:27:44. What is the man communicating by shaking his hand? (Stop talking, be quiet.)
- *Freaks and Geeks*—Episode #104
  ○ Chapter 1, from 00:08:30–00:08:50. Harris puts up his hand to say, "Stop asking because I'm not going to tell you."
  ○ Chapter 4, from 00:38:50–00:39:10. The teacher, Mr. Kowchevski, makes a hand gesture to tell people to stop talking and listen to him.

Informational Gesture Chart

Complete the section for the stop gesture on the Gestures ~ Information Chart, Appendix 6-24, including the following information.

When & where?
- To tell someone to stop moving
- To tell someone to stop what they are doing or saying

What does it mean?
- "You need to stop and stay where you are."
- "You need to stop doing that."
- "You need to stop saying that."

Shhh! & I Can't Hear You

Model and Practice

Review what the "shhh" gesture means, then cup your hand around your ear and ask what that gesture means. Explain that it not only helps the listener hear better by pulling in more sound but it also tells the speaker that he or she needs to speak louder.

Have another staff person or student talk to you, varying his or her volume. Use the "shhh" and "can't hear you" gestures to indicate when the speaker needs to speak louder or quit talking.

Pair up students and have them repeat the activity above, taking turns being the speaker. If needed, provide some text to read or phrases to repeat.

Informational Gesture Chart

Complete the "shhh" section of the chart, Appendix 6-24, including the following information:

Shhh
When & where?
- In a place where people are supposed to be quiet, such as a library or movie theater
- To tell someone to stop talking or talk quietly

What does it mean?
- "Don't talk."
- "Talk more quietly."
- "Don't make so much noise."

Can't Hear You
When & where?
- When someone needs to speak louder
- To indicate to others that you are trying to listen to the speaker

What does it mean?
- "Speak louder. I can't hear you."
- "I'm trying to listen to the speaker."

Pointing

Model and Practice

Explain that when someone points towards something, she will usually also look in that direction. Sometimes a person will use her head to point, such as nodding her head to say, "over there," or "let's go over there." Demonstrate looking at and pointing with your finger at various objects around the room, asking students to guess what you are pointing at. Look at and nod towards different items as well.

Demonstrate how pointing is different from a finger shake, and explain that using your finger to point to someone who is nearby is considered rude or threatening. To refer to someone close, it is more polite to nod at her or gesture with an open hand.

Have students sit in a circle facing each other. Have them take turns pointing to different objects in the room, using eye gaze as well. Other students try to guess what each student is pointing at.

Where Is She?

Have students stand around the room, some students close to each other and some far away. Direct questions to individual students, asking them where another student is. The student then responds by using a gesture—either pointing if the student is standing across the room, or nodding or using an open hand if standing close by.

Video Clips

- *Cool Runnings*—Chapter #8, from 00:31:42–00:32:10. What is the woman telling the man to do by pointing her finger? (Walk over there; I want to talk to you.)
- *Cool Runnings*—Chapter #8, from 00:31:30–00:31:38. What are the men saying by pointing and laughing? ("You are so funny.")
- *Uncle Nino*—Scene #7 at 00:01:27. Bones nods his head towards outside, to indicate "Let's go outside and talk."
- *Freaks and Geeks*—Episode #104, Chapter 2 from 00:21:18–00:21:48. Mr. Kowchevski, the teacher, points at Lindsay, indicating she is in trouble.

Informational Gesture Chart

Complete the pointing section of the chart, Appendix 6-24, including the following information:

When & where?
- To show where someone or something is
- To show what you are talking about
- To give directions

What does it mean?
- "The person/thing is there."
- "That is the person/thing that I'm talking about."
- "Go that way."

Shrugging

Model and Practice

Review what the shrug gesture looks like and means. Point out that shrugging involves three parts of the body. The shoulders and eyebrows are briefly raised, and sometimes the palms of the hands are turned upward.

Have students ask you a few questions that you wouldn't know the answer to (such as their favorite game or movie) and give a shrug in response. Provide questions for students to ask, if needed. As you shrug, explain that you don't know the answer.

Next, have students ask you a few questions relating to a preference or decision that you don't really care about, such as the ones below. Shrug to indicate that you don't care.

1. Do you want green beans or peas?
2. Which do you like better, maple or oak trees?
3. Do you want to go to the 1:00 or 3:00 movie?
4. Which do you like better, the blue or the green marker/pencil?
5. We could make your appointment for 10:00 or 10:30. What would you like?

Pair up students and have them take turns asking each other questions they think their partner wouldn't know, with the partner using a shrug to indicate that she doesn't know. If the student knows the answer, she gives the answer without shrugging. If the student shrugs while giving the answer, but is sure of the answer, have her repeat the answer without shrugging. Explain that when you shrug while saying something you appear to be unsure of your answer, as if you are guessing.

Ask students questions, such as the ones above, having them shrug to indicate when they don't have a preference.

Video Clips

- *How to Eat Fried Worms*—These two scenes are within a minute of each other and provide examples of two different ways a shrug is used.
  - Scene #5—00:22:00–00:22:20. Boy shrugs to express "What can I do?"
  - Scene #6—00:23:45–00:23:54. Girl shrugs as emphasis to question, "Why would you?"
- *A Christmas Story*—Scene #11, from 00:28:35–00:28:45. The deliveryman shrugs when asked what's in the box.
- *Freaks and Geeks*, Episode #106, Chapter 1, from 00:22:30-00:22:50.

Informational Gesture Chart

Complete the shrug section of the chart in Appendix 6-24, including the following information:

When & where?
- To respond to a question when you don't know the answer
- To respond to a question that calls for choice, when you don't care

What does it mean?
- "I don't know."
- "I don't care."

Counting

Model and Practice

Demonstrate how people will sometimes indicate a number between one and five by showing that number of fingers. This is particularly true when it is noisy or you need to be quiet so as not to disturb others.

Discuss how pointing one or two fingers in the air can sometimes be confusing. One finger could mean, "one," or it could be used to emphasize what is being said. Two fingers could mean, "two," or could be used as a sign for victory or peace. Relate different scenarios and how these gestures would be used, such as the following:

- I'm at a ball game and I'm ordering two cokes.
- Greeting someone with the peace sign.
- Fans cheering their team after they won, chanting, "We're number 1!"
- Kitchen worker signaling to the cook that she needs one order of fries.
- The teacher saying, "This is a really important thing to remember."

Ask students to answer some questions without saying anything. Ask simple questions that can be answered with a number between one and five, such as the following:

- What is 2 +1?
- How many fingers do you have on one hand?
- How many ears do you have?

Informational Gesture Chart

Complete the counting gesture section of the chart in Appendix 6-24, including the following information:

When & where?
- To indicate a number when the listener is looking at you
- When the listener may have a hard time hearing or understanding you
- When you are trying to be very quiet

What does it mean?
- "One," "two," or "three," or so on.

Yawning

Model and Practice

Ask students to observe as you act out the following short scenario. Have a staff person or a student read a passage from a book. Choose a passage that would hold little interest for anyone in the class. As the passage is read, gaze around the room, looking bored and yawn several times.

Discuss the following:

- A yawn may indicate boredom as well as tiredness.
- If you yawn when listening to someone speaking, he may think you are not interested in what he's saying.
- Yawning is "contagious."
- Yawning without covering your mouth is considered impolite.
- If someone is yawning when you are speaking, they may be bored and you should do one of the following:
  - Talk about something else.
  - Ask the listener a question.
  - End the conversation.

Have students sit facing each other and take turns yawning and covering their mouths. Have students observe whether they start feeling tired as they watch others yawn.

Pair up students, designating one student as the talker and one as the listener. The listener should decide at some point to look bored and begin yawning. The speaker should then change the topic, ask a question, or end the conversation. Explain that since yawning is seen as a lack of interest, when a student yawns, he may want to reassure others that he is not bored. For example, he might say, "Sorry, I didn't get much sleep last night."

Informational Gesture Chart

Complete the yawning section of the chart in Appendix 6-24, including the following information.

When & where?
- When someone is tired or sleepy
- When someone is bored

What does it mean?
- "I'm tired."
- "I'm bored."
- "I saw someone else yawning."

Winking

Model and Practice

Gather a few pictures of people winking. Photos can be easily found online at sites such as Google Images (www.google.com). Show the pictures to students and ask them to guess why the person might be winking.

- Discuss that people wink when they are in a good mood and feeling playful. A wink can have different meanings. It can mean:
  - We share a secret.
  - What I said isn't true. I am just kidding.
  - I like you.

- With adolescents, discuss that sometimes winking can be inappropriate (for example, if you are on a bus and a stranger keeps winking at you).
- Relate occasions when students have observed someone winking and what they think it meant in each situation.

Have students watch you and randomly choose students to wink at. Once a student has been winked at, have her wink back. Keep in mind that some people are physically unable to wink, but a wink can be acknowledged by smiling at the winker. Discuss that it is OK not to wink back in real-life situations. Probably the safest rule is to wink back when you understand why the person is winking at you and you know and like that person.

 ## Video Clips

- *A Christmas Story*—scene #17, from 00:46:55–00:47:38. Ralph winks at the teacher, believing that they share a secret (that she will support his efforts to get an air rifle for Christmas).
- *High School Musical*—scene #9, at 00:15:08. Start watching at 00:14:50 to help understand the situation. The girl and her brother want to change the time for the callback tryouts so they will be guaranteed to win. The girl winks at her brother, indicating they are getting what they want, and sharing a secret.

 ## Informational Gesture Chart

Complete the wink section of the chart in Appendix 6-24, including the following information.

When & where?
- When the other person is looking at you
- The other person could be close or far away
- When people are kidding around
- When people like each other

What does it mean?
- "We have a secret."
- "I'm just kidding."
- "I like you."
- "I'm flirting with you"

Additional Learning Activities

 ## Worksheets

Distribute the "What Does It Mean?" and "What Is the Listener Telling You?" worksheets from Appendix 6-26 and 6-27. Have students complete them individually or as a group.

Gesture Bingo

The game of Bingo can be played using the boards and expressions to read aloud provided in Appendix 6-28 and 6-29. A blank Bingo board is also provided in Appendix 6-30 to create additional bingo boards.

The teacher or a designated student reads the sentences aloud. Players place a marker, such as a penny, if their board shows a gesture that expresses that thought. More than one gesture may be appropriate. For example, when the caller reads, "Yes. I like that," players could place a marker on the OK gesture, the thumbs up gesture, the head nod, or even the fist bump or high five. Any reasonable answer should be accepted, but players may only place one marker per expression. Encourage discussions about what the gesture means and the feelings involved.

Homework Assignment

Have the students observe at home, school, or in the community for information gestures such as head nodding or shaking, thumbs up or down, the OK gesture, finger pointing, etc. Students report back about informational gestures they have observed.

Chapter 7

Putting It All Together

In real-life situations, we need to simultaneously read facial expressions, posture, orientation, eye gaze, personal space, and gestures, while understanding the critical role context plays. This final unit therefore includes ideas for activities to integrate the different aspects of body language, including facial expressions, to arrive at a single impression.

The following activities provide the opportunity to view the different parts of body language *altogether* and *in context*. It's essential to consider what is happening, where, and with whom in order to accurately assess what the body language means.

Helping Students Interpret Context

Explain to students that to understand someone's body language, it's often necessary to keep in mind:

- where you are,
- who you are with, and
- what is happening and what just happened before.

Worksheet: Understanding Context

Distribute and complete the "Understanding Context" worksheet from Appendix 7-1 either individually or as a group. Discuss how context makes a difference when interpreting body language. Or as an alternative, have students role-play each scenario and decide which answer is more likely.

Using Picture Books

Picture books can be particularly helpful because they present body language in context. What is happening in the story guides the child's understanding of what the character is feeling and what the body language means. Whenever you are reading a book that has pictures with your students, pause occasionally to note the body language and likely feelings of the characters. You can also read books to specifically study the body language.

Choosing Books

In choosing picture books to use, keep the following in mind:

- Choose stories that have people as the main characters and illustrations that are realistic enough that the illustrated body language can easily be equated to real-life body language.
- Choose stories that involve interactions between two or more people—stories about personal relationships and interactions.
- Choose stories about situations that the child can relate to, so he can understand the emotions behind the body language.

How to Use Books

There are various ways to use picture books. Begin by following the steps below. Once a student is familiar with the process, try one of the other methods described below.

Body Language Book Reading

1. Look at the picture on the first page.
2. Discuss the body language.
   - What do you see?
   - What do you think is happening?
   - What do you think the people are feeling?
3. Read the text on the page.
4. Discuss
   - What do you now think is happening?
   - What do you now think the people are feeling?
   - What do you think is going to happen next?
5. Continue to the next page. (You may want to simply read some pages, if there is little body language to discuss.)

Previewing the Book

(An alternative way to use picture books)

1. Look through the entire book. Without reading the text, pause frequently to guess what is happening and what will happen next.
2. Read the book.
3. Discuss differences between what you thought and what actually happened.

Hidden Pictures

(Another fun way to use books to study body language)

1. Before using the book, cover parts of key pictures with a sheet of paper or a sticky note. (Choose illustrations in which body language gives a clue as to what is under the flap, such as everyone looking with surprised expressions toward the covered area. See example on page 89.)
2. Read the book until you get to a page with a flap or sheet of paper.

3. Guess what is underneath the flap before reading the text for that page.
4. If the page with the flap has text, read it. Make changes to your guess if you want.
5. Look under the flap and describe what is happening.

Questions & Discussions

When using picture books, it usually works best to first ask the student what he thinks is taking place in the picture and what body language leads him to think that. If he has missed some of the key information provided by the body language, then point out specific body language and explore it together. For example, the following questions could be used with the illustration below.

- General question—What do you think is going on in the picture?
- Specific questions to draw out more information.

  ○ Look at the boy on the left with the dark shirt. How do you think he is feeling? (upset, sad)
  ○ What is he doing to make you think that? (head down, eyes down or closed, hand covering face)
  ○ Why do you think he feels that way? (The other boy is upset with him and is speaking to him in an angry way.)
  ○ What is the boy in the white t-shirt doing to make you think he feels that way? (angry facial expression, leaning toward the other boy, shaking his finger at him)
  ○ The boy has his finger in the air. What do you think that gesture means? (He is threatening or intimidating the other boy.)
  ○ Is the girl sitting behind them paying attention to what is happening? Why do you think so? (She is watching them.)
  ○ How do you think she is feeling? (She is upset by what is happening.)
  ○ What tells you that she feels that way? (her facial expression)

Recommended Picture Books

Picture books, graphic novels, and comic books can all be used to learn about body language. Typically, picture books are more appropriate for younger children, and graphic novels and comic books for older kids. However, what is happening in the story is the most important factor when selecting books. Can the child understand and relate to the characters and their experiences?

Below are picture books with fairly realistic illustrations, numerous examples of body language, and situations that most children in kindergarten through fifth grade can relate to. Some authors have numerous books appropriate for this purpose, and are listed by the author's name, not by individual books. Other appropriate books, which are not written by the authors listed, are listed separately.

Authors:
- Danneberg, Julie
- Finchler, Judy
- Ludwig, Trudy
- Moss, Pennie & Mike Narver
- Teague, Mark

Books:
- *Carmen Learns English* by Judy Cox
- *A Fine Fine School* by Sharon Creech
- *Nobody Knew What to Do: A Story About Bullying* by Becky Ray McCain

Using Graphic Novels and Comics

When teaching about body language in context to older students, graphic novels and comics are often more age appropriate than picture books. Graphic novels are typically geared toward older kids—upper elementary, middle school, or high school students.

Choosing Graphic Novels and Comics

Many graphic novels, and often the ones preferred by students, are full of action and incredible creatures, but have very few person-to-person interactions and little body language, other than expressions of fear. So, while there are numerous graphic novels available, many may not be useful in teaching body language.

If the child likes reading graphic novels on his own, go ahead and use what he's reading, occasionally discussing the body language that you see in the story. But in choosing graphic novels to teach body language, choose ones that involve person-to-person interactions with fairly realistic illustrations.

Using Graphic Novels and Comics

The child may not be that interested in the story, but you don't need to read the whole book, just enough to understand the purpose of the body language, sometimes only one or two frames. For example, using only two frames from *The Baby-Sitters: Kristy's Great Idea,* as in the example at the bottom of the previous page, you could ask how Kristy feels about her mother dating Watson and what body language tells you that (rolling her eyes, slumped posture, head resting in hand, sideways look).

You may choose to cover up what is being said and ask the student to guess what is happening based on body language alone, as in the example below.

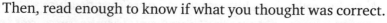

- What do you think Kristy might be saying? (She is trying to explain or convince.)
- What hints does her body language give you? (Her facial expression, orientation—facing the other girl—and her open hand gesture.)
- How does the other girl feel about what Kristy is saying? (Unsure, reluctant, resistant, doesn't want to do it.)
- What body language tells you that? (Orientation—she is not facing Kristy; eye gaze—she is not looking at Kristy; her posture is slumped and closed; and her facial expression is unhappy or worried.)

Then, read enough to know if what you thought was correct.

Authors & Series:
- Meyers, Stephanie–*Twilight: The Graphic Novel*
- Petrucha, Stephan–*Nancy Drew Graphic Novels*
- Robbins, Trina–*Chicagoland Detective Agency*
- Sterling, Rod–*Rod Sterling's Twilight Zone,* Walker Books for Young Readers
- Telgemeier, Raina–*The Baby-Sitter Club* Graphic Novels
- Tokyopop Cine-Manga–graphic depictions of movies and TV shows by various authors, including:
  - Hannah Montana
  - High School Musical

  - ○ Lizzie McGuire
  - ○ Malcolm in the Middle
  - ○ The Ultimate Buffy the Vampire Slayer
- ■ Warner, Gertrude Chandler–The Boxcar Children Graphic Novels

Books:
- ■ *Banana Sunday* by Root Nibot & Colleen Coover
- ■ *Breaking Up: A Fashion High Graphic Novel* by Aimee Friedman
- ■ *The Elsewhere Chronicles* by Nykko & Bannister
- ■ *Fame: Justin Bieber: The Graphic Novel* by Tara Broeckel Ooten
- ■ *Gary the Pirate* by Scott Christian Sava
- ■ *Hereville: How Mirka Got Her Sword* by Barry Deutsch
- ■ *The Lightning Thief: The Graphic Novel* by Rick Riordan
- ■ *Page by Paige* by Laura Lee Gulledge

Acting It Out

Using role plays and drama offers students the opportunity to put what they have been learning into practice. The following mini-skits can be used to introduce students to acting, before short plays and skits are used.

Act As If...

Write the following statements on cards or individual slips of paper. Have students draw a card and read it silently. Then, using facial expressions, posture, eye gaze, and gestures, they should stand in such a way as to demonstrate what is written. Other students can try to guess the emotion that is being portrayed.
- You think you look really good.
- You feel embarrassed because your clothes are dirty and your hair is messy.
- You did something you are very proud of.
- You said something mean, and you feel sorry.
- You are really, really tired.
- You don't want anyone to see you.
- You just received an award.
- You are feeling sad because your dog died.

Repeat the activity, having students demonstrate the above while walking.

Say It with Meaning

Write the following feeling words on the board:
- happy
- disappointed
- disgusted
- confused
- worried
- angry

Write these statements on cards or strips of paper:
- We're having tacos for lunch.
- The neighbor is at the front door.
- We're going bowling tonight.
- It's snowing outside.
- We're going to move far away.
- Is that what you're wearing?
- What happened to you?
- I didn't like what he did.
- He's coming with us.

Have a student draw a statement card and choose one of the emotions written on the board. He then reads the statement aloud, expressing the chosen emotion through body language. Then have the student read the statement again, expressing a different emotion from the list.

Tone of voice plays a huge part in expressing feelings through verbal language, and students should be encouraged to use their voices, though this has not been covered in this curriculum. But emphasize the use of facial expressions, posture, eye gaze, and gestures by having the students freeze their expressions at the end of each statement while others try to guess the emotion.

Story Telling

Read the following short skits aloud while a student or students act them out.
- You are walking down the street feeling very tired. You hear someone calling your name, but you can't see anyone. You hear your name again. Who is that? Then way off in the distance, you see your best friend.
- You are talking with another student, but he is standing too close. You don't like it. If students are too uncomfortable with having someone too close, they could pretend that the person is too close.
- You are listening to someone talk. He's been talking a long time and it's very boring. You want him to stop talking.
- Someone you don't like comes up to you and gives you a hug.
- You are sitting next to a friend on the bus. You and your friend just had a big fight and you are mad at each other.
- You are sitting on a bench waiting for your friend. No one is around. You hear a *very loud* noise! There it is again! What's happening? You're getting scared. There it is again! You get up and go home.
- You are at the movies with a friend. She keeps whispering to you, but you want to watch the movie.
- You are watching your favorite team play. They just won!
- You are eating lunch with a friend and she just sneezed and spit food out all over the table.
- You come in late to class. Everyone turns to look at you while you walk to your seat.

Using Scripts, Skits, and Short Plays

Having students act out short skits or plays is an excellent way for them to get hands-on experience reading and using body language. Many elementary reading programs include short plays, and there are numerous books of short plays and skits available for all ages. (See the resource list below.) For the purposes of teaching body language, the following suggestions may prove helpful.

- Use plays with storylines that are easily understood, not too imaginative or silly. Students need to understand what is happening and the emotions of the characters.
- You may want to begin with a familiar story or scene that the student already knows. There are short plays written for common fairy tales or folk tales. You could also write a short script from a familiar movie scene, and have students act it out.
- Choose plays that involve lots of interpersonal interactions. Body language occurs when we're interacting.
- If possible, videotape the performance and pause it at key points to examine the body language students are using. An alternative is to instruct actors to freeze during key points in the presentation.
- When the action is paused or "frozen," discuss what the characters are feeling and how their body language communicates that.

Resources for Scripts

Primary & Intermediate:

- Barchers, Suzanne I., *Readers Theatre for Beginning Readers,* grades 1-3. Teacher Ideas Press, 1993.
- Jenkins, Diana R., *Just Deal with It! Funny Readers Theatre for Life's Not-So-Funny Moments,* grades 4-8. Libraries Unlimited, 2004.
- MacDonald, Margaret Read, *The Skit Book: 101 Skits from Kids,* grades 4-8. Linnet Books, 1990.
- Pugiano, Carol, *Easy-to-Read: Folk and Fairy Tale Plays,* grades 1-3. Scholastic Professional Books, 1997.
- Shepard, Aaron, *Stories on Stage: Children's Plays for Readers Theater,* grades 1-6. Shepard Publications, 2005.
- Worthy, Jo, *Reader's Theater for Building Fluency,* grades 3-6. Scholastic Books, 2008

Secondary:

- Allen, Laurie, *Sixty Comedy Duet Scenes for Teens.* Meriwether Publishing, 2008.
- Kane, Bo, *50 Acting Scenes for Teens.* Burbank Publishing, 2010.
- Kehret, Peg, *Acting Natural.* Meriwether Publishing, 1992.
- Scriven, Maggie, *Short and Sweet Skits for Student Actors: 55 Sketches for Teens.* Meriwether Publishing, 2010.
- Stevens, Chambers, *Sensational Scenes for Teens: The Scene Study-Guide for Teen Actors!* Sandcastle Publishing, 2001.
- Ullom, Shirley, *Get in the Act.* Meriwether Publishing, 1994.

Using Art

Many students with disabilities are visual learners and could benefit from using art to help them interpret body language. In addition to looking at body language in works of art, students can engage in simple art activities even if they do not consider themselves to be artistic. Most of the activities in this section can be adapted for fine motor difficulties.

Works of Arts

Works of arts provide great examples of body language, and examining paintings for body language clues can be a fun activity. Almost any well-known piece of art can be accessed online. (Search under images on search sites such as Google or Bing.)

Among the best paintings for examining body language are those by Norman Rockwell. Books of his paintings are readily available through most libraries. *Look! Body Language in Art* by Gillian Wolfe is a book written for children pointing out examples of body language in famous paintings.

There are extensive examples of body language in art, but the following are a few you may want to use to get you started.

- *Nameless and Friendless* by Emily Mary Osborn - Look at the eye gaze and orientation of different subjects. Who is interested in what?
- *Cheating at Cards* by Georges de La tour–Figure out what's happening from eye gaze, pointing, and facial expressions.
- *Three Cronies* by Mabel Dwight–Look at orientation, facial expressions, posture, and hand gestures. Who's talking to whom and what are they feeling?
- *The Tragedy* by Picasso–Look at how posture expresses emotion.
- *Tumblers* by Picasso–Look at eye gaze and personal space.
- *The Last Supper* by Leonardo da Vinci–Lots of examples of eye gaze, body orientation, hand gestures, and facial expressions.

Create a Collage

Have students gather pictures from magazines and make collages to show different emotions. Another activity is to put different pictures together to create a scenario and then write or tell what's happening in the collage. (See example at right.)

The boy just made a basket and his mom is very proud.

Create a Picture

Students could draw or paint a picture using body language to illustrate:
- An emotion—What does a person look like when he or she is feeling sad, scared, happy, etc.?
- A specific situation–Show someone being bullied, good friends meeting, hearing strange noises at night, etc.

Create a Cartoon

Students can create simple cartoons to illustrate different types of body language. What makes a simple drawing into a cartoon is the element of exaggeration.

Begin by spending some time looking at cartoons and comic strips from newspapers or online. Note the use of talk and thought bubbles and how body language and facial expressions are exaggerated.

Demonstrate how to draw a cartoon by first selecting a scenario for your cartoon, such as a girl talking to a boy, but the boy isn't interested. Use simple line drawings or stick figures to illustrate the scenario. See example below.

Provide students with scenarios for their cartoons or have them come up with their own. The following are just a few examples of scenarios that could be used.
- Two people talking, one getting too close.
- Two people talking, with one person using a hand gesture to show agreement or disagreement.
- One person talking while the other shows various reactions (interest, surprise, disgust, etc.) using facial expressions.
- One person talking while another shows interest or disinterest by how he orients his body.
- A student bullying someone who is scared.

Some students may want to create comic strips, using a sequence of frames to tell a short story. This involves more planning, but allows for greater expression. A good resource is *Art for Kids: Comic Strips: Create Your Own Comic Strips from Start to Finish* by Art Roche.

Using Video Clips

Using short video clips from movies or television programs is an excellent way to practice reading all types of body language. The body language is viewed within context, but unlike in a real-life situation, clips can be viewed over and over and even paused to catch the expression or gesture.

Selecting Video Clips

A number of video clips have been suggested throughout this book, and there are additional selections on the following pages. These clips were selected in order to save parents and teachers time in locating appropriate videos, but there is virtually an endless variety of video that could be used.

When selecting other or additional video clips, you may want to consider the following:

- Use movies with human characters. Children may have a harder time translating the body language of animals or unusual cartoon characters.
- Choose movies with situations that are easy for the child to understand. He may not need to understand the entire storyline, but he should be able to relate to what is happening in a particular scene.
- Look for movies for and about kids interacting with other people, particularly other kids. Fanciful tales and stories about animals usually have far fewer examples of body language, though they are often the movies kids prefer. Such movies can always be watched for enjoyment, pausing to briefly comment on the body language.

Using Video Clips

When beginning to use video scenes, the general guidelines below are helpful:

- Begin with videos that are familiar to the students so that they already know the story. This allows them to concentrate on the body language instead of trying to figure out what's happening.
- Choose videos that involve exaggerated body language, such as comedies and movies made specifically for kids.
- With each selection, consider which would be more effective, sound on or off.
- Briefly discuss what is happening in the story as the scene begins. Then watch the video clip through without interruptions.
- After that, watch the clip again, this time cueing students ahead of time on what to look for. For example, "Watch the mother's facial expression after she opens the box." Pause the scene right after the body language occurs.
  - Follow up with comments on what was observed.
  - Discuss what the characters are thinking and feeling.
- Watch the scene again without interruptions.

Once students are able to recognize body language using the above steps, challenge them with some of the following changes:

- Use video clips from unfamiliar movies.
- Choose movies with subtler body language (usually geared for older audiences).
- Discuss in more detail what the characters are thinking and feeling, including:
  - The intensity of the emotion—such as annoyed versus enraged,
  - Reasons the character might feel that way,
  - How the characters' feelings relate to their own experiences.
- Don't cue students on what to watch for. Watch the clip and pause, asking students how the character feels and what kind of body language leads them to think that.
- Watch longer segments of unfamiliar movies and pause to ask students to predict what is going to happen. Continue viewing the movie to check out their predictions.
- Watch a clip with the sound off and ask students what they think is going on and why they think that. Then repeat the scene with the sound on.
- Watch a clip with the sound off. Then provide two or three possible scenarios and have students choose which they think describes what happened and what body language they saw. Then watch the scene with the sound on.

Selected Videos

All of the video clips included in this curriculum come from the following list of movies. Each is readily available on DVD, making scene selection easier. To make finding each example of body language easier, the scene or chapter number is given, along with the number of minutes into the movie. (For example, Scene #3, from 00:25:30–00:26:00 tells you to watch scene three, starting at 25 minutes and 30 seconds and going until 26 minutes into the movie.)

All of the movies are PG (except for *Freaks and Geeks,* which is not rated, as it was a TV series), so violence, sexual content, and bad language are limited. Furthermore, scenes were selected to avoid undesired content. However, it is advisable to preview each scene to make sure it is appropriate for your students. You can then choose to view it with sound off if there is undesired language. Movies were selected to appeal to different interests and age groups, while focusing on human interactions and body language. Brief descriptions and age of characters are noted.

- *Akeelah and the Bee,* PG, Lionsgate, 2000—Story of an 11-year-old girl from south Los Angeles who competes in the national spelling bee.
- *A Christmas Story,* PG, Warner Home Video, 2007—In this movie set in the 1940s, 9-year-old Ralph deals with various boyhood situations as he tries to find ways to guarantee that there will be an air rifle for him under the Christmas tree.
- *Cheaper by the Dozen,* PG, 20th Century Fox, 2003—A modern-day story of a large family.
- *Cool Runnings,* PG, Walt Disney Video, 1993—Based on a true story of a Jamaican bobsled team that competed in the 1988 Winter Olympics.

- *Freaks and Geeks: The Complete Series*, NR, Dreamworks, 2000—TV series about high school students set in 1980s. Includes some adult topics, including teenage sex, drugs, and criminal acts.
- *High School Musical*, PG, Buena Vista Home Entertainment/Disney, 2006— A story about high school students trying out for the school musical.
- *How to Eat Fried Worms*, PG, New Line Home Video—On his first day at a new school, 11-year-old Billy accepts a dare from the school bully to eat 10 worms in one day.
- *My Summer Story*, PG, MGM, 2006—Another story about 9-year-old Ralph's adventures (*A Christmas Story*), but this time set in the summer.
- *The Sandlot*, PG, 20th Century Fox, 2002—Set in the 1960s, this movie features a fifth-grade boy named Scotty who has moved to a new town. Scotty seeks out friends at the sandlot, where neighborhood boys play baseball, although he cannot even throw a baseball.
- *Sandlot 2*, PG, 20th Century Fox, 2005—Story of kids playing baseball at the local sandlot in current day setting.

What Does It Mean?

The following short clips show different types of body language. Watch each scene and have students try to figure out the meaning of the body language.

Sandlot 2
- Scene 2, from 00:07:55–00:08:15
  - Girl rolling eyes (She's thinking, considering.)
  - Hands together in begging gesture (Please let us use your hose.)
- Scene 6, from 00:25:00–00:25:30. What is David expressing by crossing his arms and turning his back to the others? (He disagrees.)
- Scene 7, from 00:28:00–00:28:20. Palms out (OK. OK. I'm in control now.)

High School Musical
- Scene #2, from 00:10:00 to 00:10:14. Why did the girl raise her hand? (To indicate that she was Kala.)
- Scene #9, from 16:00 to 16:07. What did it mean when all the kids put their hands on top of each other's hands? (They all agreed to work together.)

Freaks and Geeks
- Episode #106, Chapter 1, from 00:06:00–00:06:50. Watch the facial expressions of the three boys as the new girl walks to her desk. What do you see and how do they feel about the new girl? (Eye contact, smiling, and eyebrow flashes–they like what they see and want to get to know her.)
- Episode #107, Chapter 1, from 00:06:38–00:07:00. Gordon does not smell good. Watch for the students' body language that shows their reaction. (Disgusted facial expression, covering nose with hand, walking away from him.)

- Episode #108
  - Chapter 1, from 00:09:05–00:09:14. Watch Neil's eyebrows. What is he communicating? (He didn't like what Bill said.)
  - Chapter 2, from 00:16:30–00:16:38. What hand gesture did Daniel use and what does it mean? (Hands together in a begging gesture, to add emphasis.)
  - Chapter 3, from 00:28:10–00:28:26. What gesture does Sam use twice? What is it communicating? (Sam shrugs twice, to say, "I don't know.")
- Episode #110
  - Chapter 3, from 00:20:37–00:20:42. What does Lindsay's smile tell you about how she is feeling? (She is not happy, not being sincere.)
  - Chapter 3, from 00:26:36–00:26:43. Are the three girls laughing with Sam or at Sam? How can you tell? (Sam is not laughing; girls covering their mouths.)
- Episode #113
  - Chapter 4, from 00:35:40–00:35:52. Watch how Bill turns his body when the PE teacher gets into the car. What is Bill communicating? (Bill does not want to talk with him.)
  - Chapter 4, from 00:38:30–00:38:40. Watch Nick's facial expressions. How does he really feel about the boy breaking his guitar? (He's very angry.)

How to Eat Fried Worms
- Scene #2, from 00:03:55–00:04:03. Watch the scene with sound on and note the fingers held up to make a cross. Based on the context, guess what the gesture means.
- Scene #2, from 00:04:54–00:05:45. Watch for the body language the group of boys use when they see Billy, the new boy at school. Note their posture, eye gaze, orientation, and personal space. What are they expressing with their body language?

Christmas Story
- Scene 11, from 00:30:00–00:33:28.
  - Describe the father's body language. What does it tell you about how he feels about the prize? (Smiling, open posture, and open hand and arm gestures tell you he is pleased and excited.)
  - Describe the mother's body language and what it tells you about how she feels. (Frowning, making fists, fidgeting with hands tells you she doesn't like her husband's prize.)
  - Describe the mother's body language when she is standing at the window and what it tells you about how she feels. (Hunching over, a shy wave, turning her face away, and covering her face tells you she's embarrassed.)

Akeelah and the Bee
- Scene 6, from 00:25:35–00:25:55. Before Akeelah says anything, how does she try to communicate that she wants her sister to take the baby out? (Facial expression and eye gaze.)

- Scene 20, from 01:30:45–01:31:40.
  - How do most of the people show how they feel about Akeelah getting the answer right? (Smiling, cheering, clapping, hugging.)
  - How is the man (Dylan's father) feeling and what body language tells you that? (His rigid posture, crossed arms, and angry facial expression tell you he is nervous and not happy.)

The Sandlot
- Scene 7, from 00:18:30–00:19:40. (You may want to view this scene with the sound turned off to avoid some language you wouldn't want repeated. The body language gets the message across.) How do the team members express their feelings when Scotty doesn't catch the ball and hands it to the pitcher? (Surprised facial expressions, shaking head, looking down.)
- Scene 11, from 00:38:50–00:41:30.
  - When the boy is receiving mouth-to-mouth and looks at his friends, what is he communicating to his friends? (That he is fine, and he is playing a trick on the girl.)
  - Describe the girl's body language when the boy is looking at her through the fence. (She smiles and waves at him.) What does it usually mean when someone smiles while they are shaking their head? (They don't like what the person did, but they are not angry.)
- Scene 13, from 00:44:36–00:46:40.
  - How do the boys on Benny's team feel about the other boys? What body language tells you that? (They don't like them, as shown by angry facial expressions, throwing mitts on the ground, direct, confrontational orientation, hands on hips, wide stance, fists in the air.)
  - How did the team members show Hamilton Porter that they liked what he did? (Patting him on the back.)

Mixed Signals

Watch for confusing body language signals in the following clips, and discuss what the character is probably feeling.

Freaks and Geeks
- Episode #100, Chapter 2, from 00:20:06–00:20:17. The PE teacher says, "Sit down you knucklehead," while smiling and patting the student on the back. He is punishing the student, yet showing that he is pleased with the student at the same time.
- Episode #104, Chapter 1, from 00:03:53–00:04:04. The student gives a thumbs up and then makes a face, showing insincerity.
- Episode #106, Chapter 4, from 00:41:28–00:42:30. Eyes aren't smiling. He is actually feeling sad.
- Episode #116, Chapter 3, from 00:26:30–00:26:45. What is Cindy actually feeling when she says, "Yeah. I guess so?"

Cool Runnings
- Chapter 12, from 01:05:40–01:06:02. When Irv says, "Oh goody," is he really glad about what was said? What does his body language communicate?
- Chapter 13, from 01:12:16–01:12:50. As Irv was talking on the phone, did he look like he was getting good news or bad? Was the news actually good or bad news? What was going on? (Irv was playing a joke, pretending to be sad.)

Using Games to Teach Body Language

Games are a great way to combine learning about body language while practicing social skills such as turn-taking and good sportsmanship. The following games can be adapted to meet different learning abilities.

 ## Emotions Game

Use some of the facial expressions cards depicting emotions that you created in Chapter 2. Or look for emotions cards in special education or speech catalogs. Place the cards face down or in a bag. Have students take a card, identify the emotion, and make up a short scenario about why the person in the picture feels that way.

 ## Emotions Charade

Write a different emotion word on a set of index cards or use cards that depict emotions from the activity above. Each player, in turn, then draws a card and expresses the emotion using body language, while the other players try to guess. To make the game more competitive, divide students into pairs or teams. Have them take turns trying to guess the emotions of their teammate(s). Teams score points for guessing correctly within a specified time period.

 ## Body Language Telephone

This game also needs a set of cards with emotion words or pictures on them. Begin by having students line up, all facing the same direction. The last person in line, player #1, draws a card, then taps the player ahead of him, player #2, on the shoulder. When player #2 turns around, player #1 expresses the emotion through body language. Without saying anything, player #2 taps player #3 on the shoulder and imitates the body language he observed. Play continues until it's the last player's turn. All players look at the last player's expression and then watch as the first player repeats the expression he gave to start the game. Players try to guess the emotion, then player #1 reveals what was on the card.

What Are You Thinking? Charades

This game requires some more advanced skills, including reading and expressing a thought using nonverbal language.

Each player is given a copy of the "What Are You Thinking?" game board from Appendix 7-2. Create draw cards by making an extra copy of the game board and cutting it apart. A blank game board is also provided in Appendix 7-3 so you can create additional game boards with different thoughts.

Player #1 draws a card and without revealing what is on the card, uses body language to express the thought. No verbal language is allowed. The other players refer to their charts and guess what is being expressed. The player who guesses the correct answer first may then take a turn, or play can continue in a designated order.

At first, you may want to cut the game boards in half so there are only eight choices, instead of sixteen.

Conclusion

Understanding body language plays a crucial role in how we navigate our world. It is an extremely complex subject, yet one we are often expected to learn on our own. This curriculum has covered the basics, but for our children to truly integrate and use what they have learned, they will need continual coaching and practice. Everyday life will present them with endless opportunities to practice, but without continued support, these opportunities can become overwhelming.

Continue to point out examples of body language and encourage your child or students to try to interpret body language. Make it into a game. Interpreting body language can be a part of watching a movie or reading a story. Look for body language in pictures or photos in all types of media. Look for it in everyday life. Opportunities abound. Have fun as you explore the world of body language together.

Appendix

Chapter 3 Activity Pages

name_____

Relaxed and Tense Postures #1

Relaxed

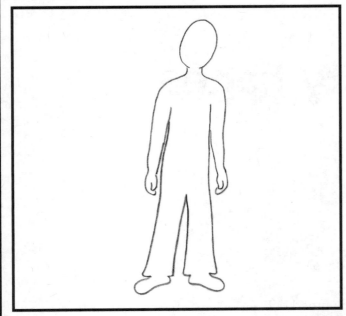

What does it look like?

How is the person feeling?

Tense

What does it look like?

How is the person feeling?

Feeling Faces

 happy  sad  angry  scared  neutral

 happy  sad  angry  scared  neutral

 happy  sad  angry  scared  neutral

 happy  sad  angry  scared  neutral

 happy  sad  angry  scared  neutral

 happy  sad  angry  scared  neutral

Reprinted from: Pat Crissey, *Getting the Message: Learning to Read Facial Expressions* (Verona, WI: Attainment Company, 2007).

name_____

Name the Posture - Tense or Relaxed #1

tense

relaxed

tense

relaxed

name_____

Open and Closed Postures #2

Open

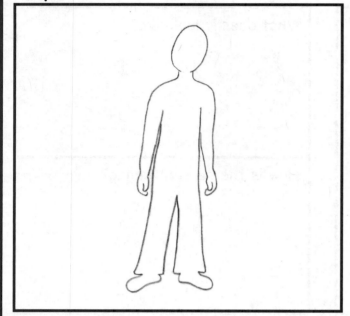

What does it look like?
How is the person feeling?

Closed

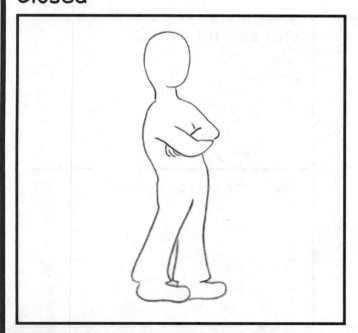

What does it look like?
How is the person feeling?

name_____

Open and Closed Postures #3

Open

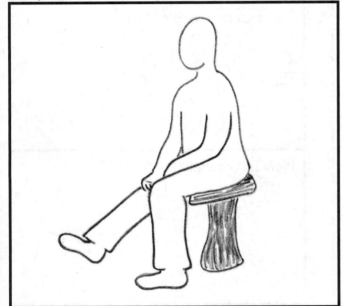

What does it look like?
How is the person feeling?

Closed

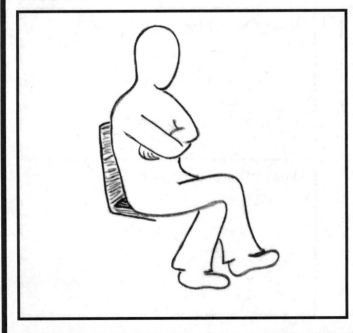

What does it look like?
How is the person feeling?

name_____

Name the Posture - Open & Closed #2

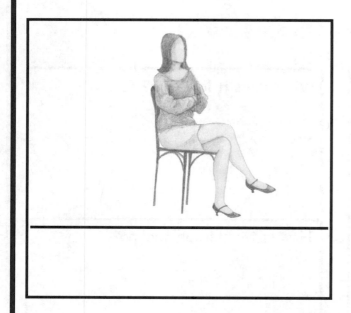

open

closed

open

closed

name_____

Expanded and Slumped Postures #4

Expanded

What does it look like?

How is the person feeling?

Slumped

What does it look like?

How is the person feeling?

name_____

Expanded and Slumped Postures #5

Expanded

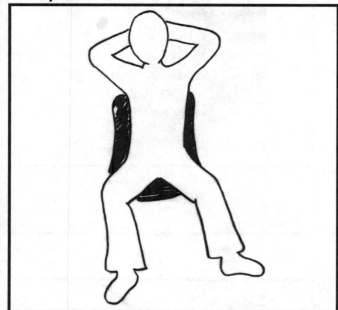

What does it look like?
How is the person feeling?

Slumped

What does it look like?
How is the person feeling?

name_____

Name the Posture - Expanded & Slumped #3

expanded	slumped
expanded	slumped

name_____

Towards and Away Postures #6

Towards

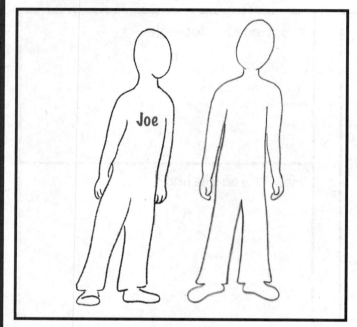

| What does it look like? |
| How is Joe feeling? |

Away

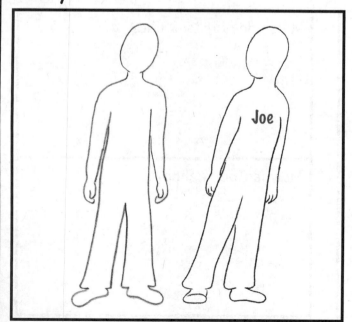

| What does it look like? |
| How is Joe feeling? |

name_____

Leaning Towards #7

Towards & Open

What does it look like?
How is Joe feeling?

Towards & Expanded

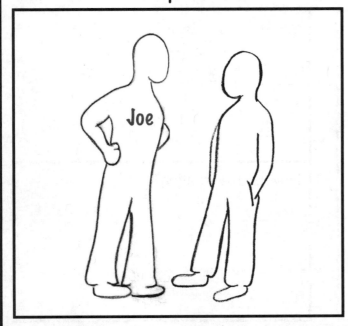

What does it look like?
How is Joe feeling?

name_____

Towards and Away Postures #8

Towards & Closed

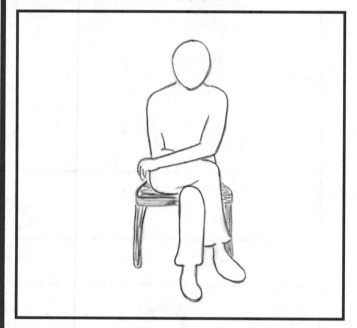

What does it look like?
How is the person feeling?

Forward & Closed

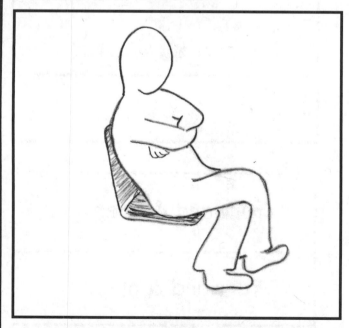

What does it look like?
How is the person feeling?

name_____

Name the Posture - Towards & Away #4

forward & expanded

away & closed

forward & open

forward & open

name_____

How Are They Feeling? #1

Directions: Write or glue the feeling word that goes with each picture.

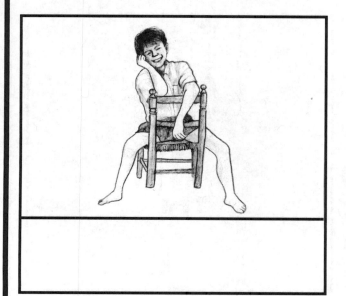

relaxed	tense
relaxed	tense

name_____

How Are They Feeling? #2

Directions: Write or glue the feeling word that goes with each picture.

angry

sad

scared

happy

name_____

How Are They Feeling? #3

Directions: Write or glue a feeling word that goes with each picture.

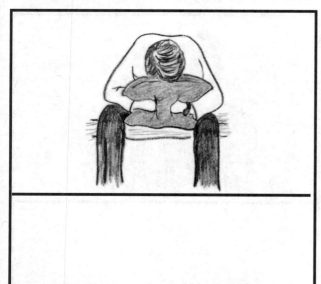

cold
scared

sad
relaxed

name_____

What Are They Thinking? #4

Directions: Write or glue what the people in each picture are thinking.

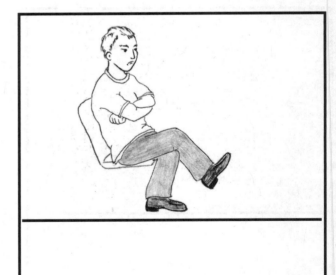

We like each other.

I'm interested in
what you are saying.

I don't want to do it
and you can't make me.

I feel so bad about what
I did. I really blew it.

Act It Out—Postures

Copy and cut apart the following scenarios.

Role Play #1

The scene: Actors #1 and #2 are watching a football game. #1's team just won and #2's team just lost.

Actor #1: Game over! Yes! We're number 1! We're number 1!

Actor #2: Yeah, I know. Don't rub it in.

Role Play #2

The scene: Actor #2 is sitting looking very sad when actor #1 walks up and sees him.

Actor #1: You look really down. What's the matter?

Actor #2: You know my dog, Max? He died last night.

Role Play #3

The scene: Actor #1 and #2 are sitting next to each other eating lunch.

Actor #1: You want to know a secret?

Actor#2: Yeah! What is it?

Role Play #4

The scene: Actor #2 is sitting and playing a video game. He is in a bad mood and doesn't want to be bothered. Actor #1 wants actor #2 to play with him.

Actor #1: Hey, you want to do something?

Actor #2: No.

Actor #1: Oh, come on. Let's go shoot some baskets.

Actor #2: No! I don't want to. Leave me alone.

Role Play #5

The scene: Actors #1 and #2 are walking in the hall. #2 accidentally bumps into #1.

Actor #1: Hey, jerk! You want my fist in your face?

Actor#2: Hey, take it easy. It was an accident.

Role Play #6

The scene: Actor #1 and #2 are sitting taking a test. #1 is getting upset because the test is too hard. #2 thinks the test is easy. He finishes it and turns it in.

Neutral Face Mask

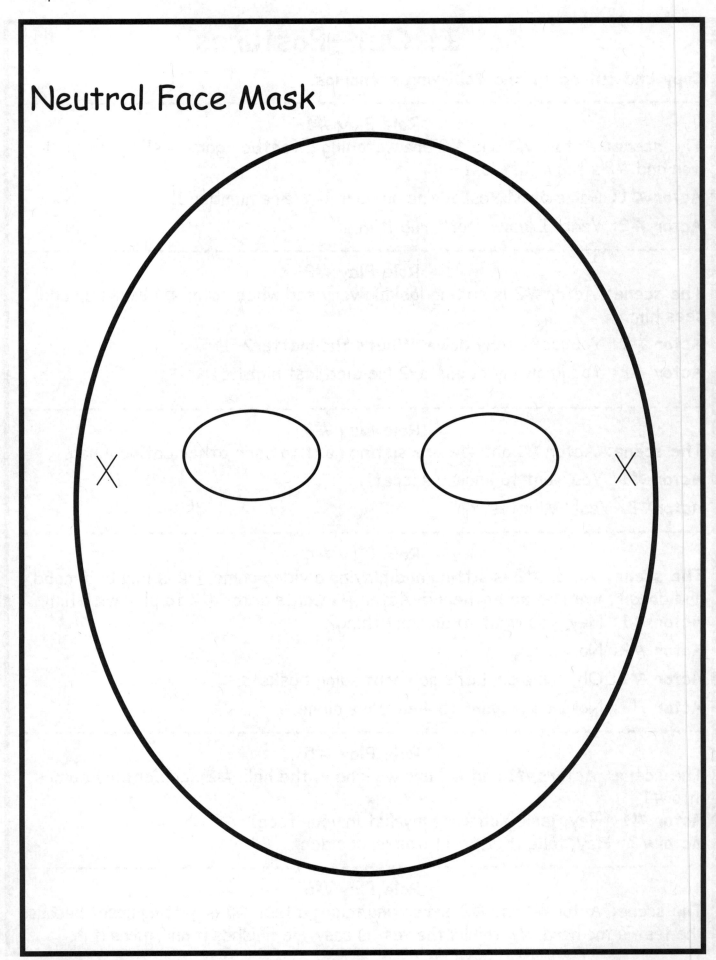

Changing Posture Flipbook

1. Color pictures in boxes at bottom of the page
2. Cut out picture boxes along dotted lines.
3. Staple or tape the 2 pictures together.

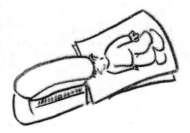

4. Use a pencil to curl the top page.
5. Roll the pencil back and forth quickly to make the man move.

Body and Face Match-up

Directions: Cut out the faces and glue them onto the matching posture.

name _____

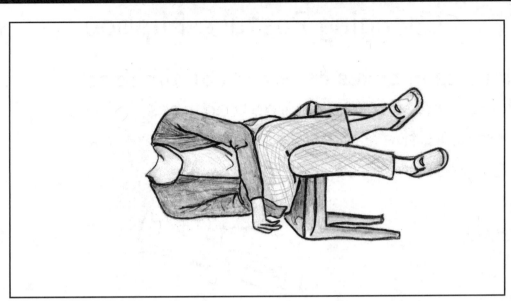

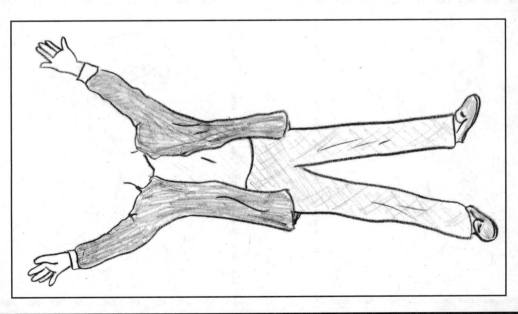

Read the Scene - Posture

Directions: Look at the pictures and check all the correct statements.

name _____

1. Who looks angry?
   - ____ a. the boy on the left
   - ____ b. the boy in the middle
   - ____ c. the girl on the right

2. Who is the girl interested in talking to?
   - ____ a. the boy on the left
   - ____ b. the boy in the middle

3. Who is the boy on the left interested in talking to?
   - ____ a. the boy in the middle
   - ____ b. the girl on the right

4. You are talking to these girls.
   - ____ a. They are interested in what you are saying.
   - ____ b. They are angry at you.
   - ____ c. They are not interested in what you are saying.

5. A good thing for you to do would be to...
   - ____ a. continue to talk to them.
   - ____ b. talk about something else.
   - ____ c. tell them you'll see them later.

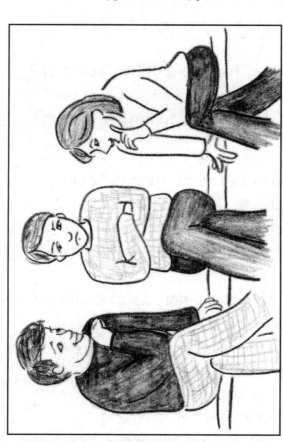

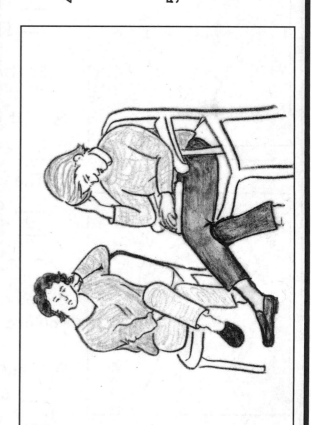

Unit Quiz - Posture

name_____

Directions: Check all correct answers or write <u>yes</u> or <u>no</u>

1. The woman in the picture is feeling...
____ a. angry.
____ b. sad.
____ c. scared.

2. What do you think her posture is telling you?
____ a. she is glad to see you.
____ b. she is mad at you.

3. Is it a good time to ask her for a favor?_____

4. You are talking with this man. Which of the following are probably true?
____ a. He is interested in what you are saying.
____ b. He is upset with you.
____ c. He is not paying attention.

5. Is it a good time to ask him for help?_____

6. Is it OK to keep on talking with him? _____

7. The woman in the picture is feeling...
____ a. angry.
____ b. sad.
____ c. scared.

8. You are talking to her. Is she interested in what you are saying? _____

9. What should you do?
____ a. Keep on talking
____ b. Ask her what is wrong.
____ c. Stop talking and leave her alone.

Appendix

Chapter 4 Activity Pages

Body Pointing Figures (Set 1)

Set 1

Roy

Jake

Body Pointing Figures (Set 2)

Set 2

Roy

Jake

Understanding Body Pointing

Away	Towards

Read the Scene - Body Pointing #1

Directions: Look at the pictures and check all the correct statements.

name _____

1. The two women are...
   _____ a. talking about something private and important.
   _____ b. are having a friendly conversation.
   _____ c. want to know what the man thinks.

2. The man is...
   _____ a. interested in what the women are saying.
   _____ b. not interested in the women's conversation.
   _____ c. is interested in something else.

3. Would it be OK to join the women's conversation?
   _____ a. Yes.
   _____ b. No, you should wait.

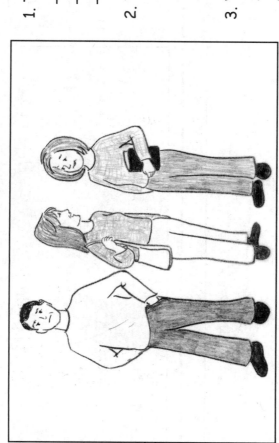

4. The man and woman are...
   _____ a. having a friendly conversation.
   _____ b. talking about something private and important.

5. The man is...
   _____ a. interested in what the woman is saying.
   _____ b. is not interested in what the woman is saying.
   _____ c. is upset with what the woman is saying.

6. Would it be OK to join this conversation?
   _____ a. Yes.
   _____ b. No, you should wait.

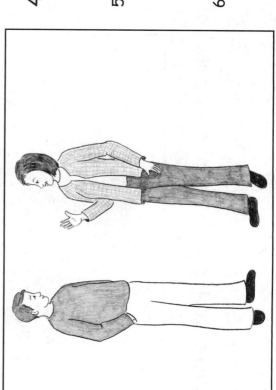

Read the Scene - Body Pointing #2

name _____

Directions: Look at the pictures and check all the correct statements.

1. This boy and girl are...
   ___ a. talking about something private and important.
   ___ b. are having a friendly conversation.
   ___ c. showing that they don't want anyone to join them.

2. The girl is...
   ___ a. not really interested in what the boy is saying.
   ___ b. interested in what the boy is saying.
   ___ c. is watching for her friend to show up.

3. Would it be OK to join the couple's conversation?
   ___ a. Yes.
   ___ b. No, you should wait.

4. The two men are...
   ___ a. having a friendly conversation.
   ___ b. talking about something private and important.
   ___ c. interested in what they are talking about.
   ___ d. not interested in what they are talking about.
   ___ e. angry with each other.
   ___ f. having an argument.

5. Would it be a good time to join their conversation?
   ___ a. Yes.
   ___ b. No, you should wait.

Eye Gaze Faces

Set 1

Set 2

Read the Scene - Eye Gaze #1

name _____

Directions: Look at the pictures and check all the correct statements.

1. The teacher seems to be...
   ___ a. interested in the boy and what he's doing.
   ___ b. interested in what is going on across the room.
   ___ c. waiting to hear what the boy has to say.

2. The boy...
   ___ a. looks interested in what the teacher is thinking.
   ___ b. is showing that he does not want to talk.
   ___ c. is feeling troubled.

3. Would it be OK to go talk to the teacher right now?
   ___ a. Yes.
   ___ b. No, you should wait.

4. The boy...
   ___ a. is interested in what is happening across the room.
   ___ b. is mad at the girl.
   ___ c. wants to talk with the girl.

5. The girl...
   ___ a. does not know the boy is standing there.
   ___ b. knows the boy is talking to her.
   ___ c. really wants to talk to the boy.

6. Would it be OK to join this conversation?
   ___ a. Yes.
   ___ b. No, you should wait.

Read the Scene - Eye Gaze #2

Directions: Look at the pictures and check all the correct statements.

name _____

1. The woman is...
   ____ a. very interested in what the man is saying.
   ____ b. is interested in what is on the paper.
   ____ c. may not know the man is talking to her.

2. The man...
   ____ a. may be talking about what is on the paper.
   ____ b. is angry at the woman and wants her to go away.

3. Would it be OK to go talk to these people right now?
   ____ a. Yes.
   ____ b. No, you should wait.

4. The man who is sitting....
   ____ a. does not know the other man is there.
   ____ b. is upset and does not want to talk.
   ____ c. is happy to see the other man.
   ____ d. is probably thinking about the other man.

5. The man who is standing...
   ____ a. is happy to see the other man.
   ____ b. is upset.

6. Would it be OK to go up and talk to these men right now?
   ____ a. Yes.
   ____ b. No, you should wait.

Understanding Eye Contact

Too much eye contact	Avoids eye contact	Makes eye contact

Conversation Scripts

Conversation Script #1

Actor #1: Are you doing anything after school on Friday?

Actor #2: No, nothing special. Why?

Actor #1: Do you want to come over to my house? We're ordering pizza and we could play some games or something.

Actor #2: Sure, that sounds good. Did you check it out with your parents?

Actor #1: Yeah. They said it would be fine. I have to get my homework done first, though.

Actor #2: How long does that usually take you?

Actor #1: Not that long on Friday. Teachers don't give that much for over the weekend.

Actor #2: I always put my homework off until Sunday night, so you can call me on Friday when you get it done.

Actor #1: Yeah. I'll give you a call. Should be around 4:30 or so.

Actor #2: Okay.

- -

Conversation Script #2

Actor #1: Don't you ever buy your lunch at school?

Actor #2: No. I don't like most of their lunches. I guess I'm kind of picky.

Actor #1: Don't you get tired of peanut butter and jelly sandwiches?

Actor #2: Not really. I like them. Do you actually like the hamburgers they have here? They look awful.

Actor #1: Oh, they're okay. Nothing special, but better than peanut butter and jelly everyday. Don't you ever eat hamburgers, like at a hamburger place?

Actor #2: I usually get chicken nuggets. And I like pizza, but not the pizza they serve here. It's gross. Do you eat, like everything?

Actor #1: Not everything. I don't like a lot of vegetables, like broccoli, and carrots, and spinach. Yuck!

Actor #2: Yeah. Me either.

Ending a Conversation

Signals	What does it mean?	What do I do?

Role Plays—Ending a Conversation

Role Play #1 – With Prompts

Directions: Actor #2 silently reads the words inside the brackets [ ] and does what they say.

Actor #1: Hey, did you get to go to the movies this weekend?

Actor #2: No. Did you?

Actor #1: Yeah. It was a great movie! You've got to see it.

Actor #2: Yeah, I want to see it. I didn't have any money to go last weekend, but I'm planning to go this coming weekend. *[look away]*

Actor #1: Wait until you see how it ends. It's awesome! The main guy is…

Actor #2: Don't tell me what happens. I'm going to see it. *[turn away and look away]*

Actor #1: There were a lot of people there. The theater was full. The line was really long to get in.

Actor #2: I'm definitely going to see it. I've got to get going. See you later. *[turn and walk away]*

Actor #1: Yeah, bye.

Role Play #2 – Without Prompts

Directions: Actor #2 adds "end of conversation" signals where they would likely go.

Actor #1: Hey, how did you do on the test?

Actor #2: I'm not sure. I think I did OK.

Actor #1: That was so hard!

Actor #2: Yeah, there were some parts that I wasn't sure about.

Actor #1: And I really studied for it too. Did you study a lot?

Actor #2: Yeah, quite a bit, I guess.

Actor #1: I just hope I passed it.

Actor #2: Yeah, me too. I need to get to class. See you later.

Actor #1: Yeah, see you later.

Snapshot Scenarios

Show how you would be standing if someone took a snapshot of you and your partner in the following situations.

1. Person #1 is telling person #2 a secret.

2. Person #1 and person #2 just met. They are talking to each other during free time.

3. Person #1 and person #2 are talking about someone who is on the other side of the room.

4. Person #1 and person #2 are having an argument.

5. Person #1 is listening while person #2 explains a math problem.

6. Person #1 and person #2 are talking about something that is private.

7. Person #1 is mad at person #2. Person #2 is trying to explain what happened.

8. Person #1 is talking to the teacher (person #2) about a problem he/she is having.

I Spy Lotto

	Free	

name_____

What's Happening?

Look at the picture and answer the questions below.

Check the answer that is most likely.
1. The cake is for...
_____ a. Alex.
_____ b. Kelly.
_____ c. Lisa.

2. What is Lisa thinking?
_____ a. "It makes me feel good to get this cake."
_____ b. "I don't understand. Who is the cake for?"
_____ c. "Cakes are really boring."

3. What is Kelly thinking?
_____ a. "I hope Alex likes the cake."
_____ b. "This cake looks really good."
_____ c. "Lisa is smiling. I think she likes the cake."

Activity Sheet #1

name_____

What Are They Looking At?

Draw eyes for the people in the picture to show what they are looking at.

1. **Jeff** is looking at **Amanda**.

2. **Amanda** is looking at **Amy**.

3. **Jenny** is looking at **Amy**.

4. **Amy** is looking at the **ice cream cone**.

Activity Sheet #3

name_____

Tell What's Going On

Cut and glue the sentences below that match each picture.

They are looking at the same thing.

They are having a friendly talk.

They are mad at each other.

They are talking about something private.

name_____

Reading Body Language

Look at the picture and answer the questions below.

1. Who is talking?
____ a. Amy
____ b. Doug
____ c. Laura
____ d. Annie

2. Who is interested in what is being said?
____ a. Amy and Doug
____ b. Laura, Annie, and Doug
____ c. Laura and Annie

3. Who is not interested in what is being said?
____ a. Amy
____ b. Doug
____ c. Annie

4. How can you tell that person is not interested? _____
_____
_____

Activity Sheet #4

Unit Quiz—Body Orientation and Eye Gaze

Directions: Check all the answers that are true.

1. The people in this picture are...
    a. Talking about something important.
    b. Having a friendly conversation.
    c. Not interested in what each other is saying.

2. When you are talking with someone you should look at his or her face...
    a. All the time.
    b. On and off.
    c. A little over half of the time.

3. You can tell it's your turn to talk when the person...
    a. Pauses and looks at you.
    b. Pauses and looks to the side.
    c. Says, "What do you think?"

4. When the person you are talking to keeps looking away, it probably means...
    a. He is not interested in what you're saying.
    b. He wants to end the conversation.
    c. He is interested in what you're saying.

(continued)

5. The people in this picture are...
   a. Talking about something important.
   b. Having a friendly conversation.
   c. Not interested in what each other is saying.

6. When someone turns his body away from a person who is talking to him, it may mean...
   a. He is finished talking and wants to leave.
   b. He doesn't know the person is talking to him.
   c. He is paying attention and interested.

7. When someone stares at a person, that person usually thinks that...
   a. The other person is angry.
   b. The other person is being friendly.
   c. The other person is being a bully.

8. Someone might be looking away during a conversation because...
   a. He or she needs to take time to think.
   b. He or she wants to end the conversation.
   c. Because the person feels shy or embarrassed.

Appendix

Chapter 5 Activity Pages

- 5-1 What's Personal Space? Role Plays
- 5-2 Personal Space
- 5-3 Too Close—What Does It Mean?
- 5-4 Inside a Personal Space Bubble
- 5-5 In a Crowd
- 5-6 Different Kinds of Touching Role Plays
- 5-7 OK Types of Touch
- 5-8 *Not* OK Types of Touch
- 5-9 Where to Touch
- 5-10 Create a Scene
- 5-11 Too Close, Too Far, Just Right Role Plays
- 5-12 Personal Space Story
- 5-13 Personal Space
- 5-14 Where Would You Sit?
- 5-15 Touching
- 5-16 Read the Body Language
- 5-17 Read the Body Language—Part 2
- 5-18 Unit Quiz—Personal Space and Touching

What's Personal Space? Role Plays

Scene: actor 2 standing while actor 1 walks up.

Actor 1 *[walks up to within 12 inches of actor 2]*: Hey! How's it going with you?

Actor 2 *[backing away]*: Oh, pretty good. What are you up to?

Actor 1 *[walking closer]*: I just got a new video game and I'm heading home to play it. Want to come over?

Actor 2 *[backing away]*: I don't think I can. I really should go home and do my homework. I'll see you later.

- -

Scene: lunch table with 2 chairs side by side.

Actor 1 *[sitting at a table eating lunch]*: Hi, want to sit here?

Actor 2 *[pushes empty chair very close to actor 1 and sits down and starts eating lunch]*: Thanks. I'm starved. I hate having the late lunch, don't you?

Actor 1 *[moving chair away from actor 2]*: Yeah. I get pretty hungry.

Actor 2 *[moving chair closer]*: How do you think you did on the test this morning?

Actor 1 *[getting up]*: I think I did OK. Well, I'm finished. I'll see you later.

Personal Space

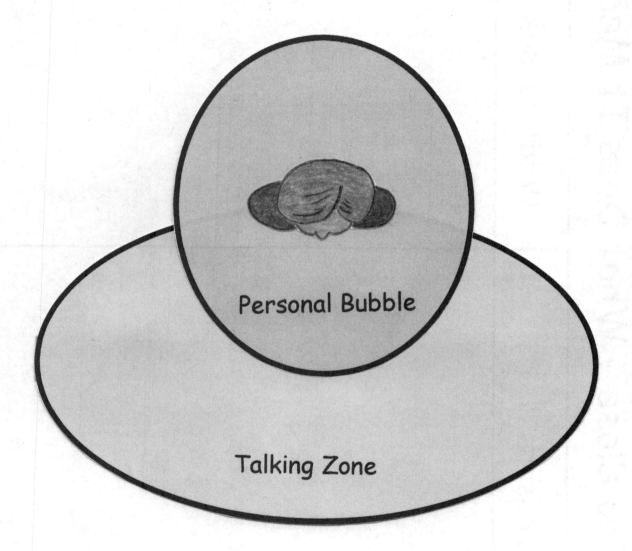

Personal Bubble

Talking Zone

Reprinted from: Pat Crissey, *Teaching Communication Skills to Children with Autism* (Verona, WI: Attainment Company, 2009).

Too Close – What Does It Mean?

What to look for	Possible reasons

Inside a Personal Space Bubble

Who	What happens

name_____

In a Crowd

Check all the sentences that tell what people usually do when they are in a crowded place.

____ Sit or stand still.

____ Look at all the people around them.

____ Talk to the person next to them.

____ Look down or stare off into space.

____ Look at a book or magazine.

____ Say "hi" to everyone.

____ Have a blank look on their faces.

____ Walk around a lot.

____ Smile a lot.

____ Keep arms and legs close to their bodies, not spread out.

Different Kinds of Touching Role Plays
(Real names can be substituted.)

Scene: Ted and Steve are friends walking together and they meet Jake.

Ted *[speaking to Jake]*: Hi, Jake. How's it going?

Jake: Oh, pretty good.

Ted: Do you know my friend Steve?

Jake: No. Hi, Steve.

Steve *[gives Jakes a hug]*: Hi, Jake.

- -

Scene: Maria and Tina are standing together talking. Jamal walks up to them.

Jamal: Hey Tina! How are things?

Tina: Really good. Do you two know each other? Maria, this is Jamal.

Jamal *[puts out his hand to shake hands]*: Hi, Maria.

Maria *[shakes Jamal's hand]*: Hi, Jamal.

- -

Scene: Andy is sitting right in front of Josh on the bus. Andy drops a paper out of his notebook, but doesn't notice.

Josh *[picks up the paper and taps Andy on the shoulder]*: You dropped this.

Andy *[takes paper]*: Oh, thanks.

- -

Scene: Carlos is standing in line behind Haley.

Carlos *[touches Haley's hair]*: You have really soft hair.

Haley *[pulls her head away]*: Don't.

Carlos *[touches her hair again]*: I just like touching it. It's so soft.

- -

Scene: Ryan walks up to Derrick.

Ryan: I heard that you won 1st prize.

Derrick: Yeah, can you believe it?

Ryan *[giving Derrick a pat on the back]*: That's great. Congratulations!

OK Types of Touch

Type	With Whom	Why	How

Not OK Types of Touch

Types	What to Do

name_____

Where to Touch

Write the number and draw an arrow to show where to touch someone.

 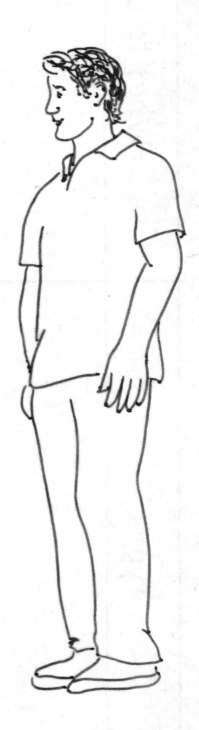

Create a Scene

Draw or cut out pictures of people and place them how they should be standing in each of the following scenarios.

- -

Two people who just met each other for the first time are talking to each other.

- -

Two close friends are talking about something private and they do not want other people to hear what they are saying.

- -

Four people who don't know each other are standing in line.

- -

Three friends are standing and talking to each other.

- -

A student is asking the teacher a question about a homework assignment.

Too Close, Too Far, Just Right Role Plays

Act out each role play three times—first standing too close, then too far away, and the third time stand in the talking zone.

Actor 1: Want to shoot some hoops?

Actor 2: Not right now. I'm really tired. I didn't get much sleep last night.

Actor 1: How come?

Actor 2: My brother was coughing all night and kept me awake.

- -

Student: I did my homework, but I can't find it.

Teacher: Do you still have your homework folder?

Student: Yeah, but it's not in it.

Teacher: Well, you can do it during free time.

- -

Actor 1: Are you doing anything Saturday afternoon?

Actor 2: I don't think so. Why?

Actor 1: I want to go to the movie at the shopping center. I thought maybe you could meet me there.

Actor 2: I'll check with my mom and let you know tomorrow. OK?

Personal Space Story

Everyone has an invisible bubble around them. You can't see it, but it's their personal space bubble.

People want other people to stay outside of their personal space bubble most of the time.

Moms and dads and kids sometimes like to hug or sit really close together and that's OK. But other people don't like it when I get too close to them. It makes them feel funny.

I can remember not to get too close to other people by thinking about their personal space bubbles. If I put my arm out, that is how close I can get to someone.

If a kid steps away from me or makes a mad face, I am probably standing too close.

Kids will feel a lot better if I remember not to get too close. Kids will like being with me more if I remember their personal space bubbles.

Reprinted from: Pat Crissey, *Teaching Communication Skills to Children with Autism* (Verona, WI: Attainment Company, 2009).

Activity Sheet #1

name_____

Personal Space

Cut and glue the sentences below that match each picture.

| They are too close together. They look angry. | They are standing in the talking zone having a friendly talk. |

| They are too far apart to have a friendly talk. | They are standing in the talking zone having a friendly talk. |

name_____

Where Would You Sit?

Read about each picture and put an **X** on the chair you would sit on.

You are at the doctor's office. These are the only empty chairs. You do not know the man reading the paper.

You are at the doctor's office. These are the only empty chairs. You do not know these people.

You are at the doctor's office. These are the only empty chairs. This boy is a friend of yours.

Activity Sheet #2

name_____

Touching

Write **OK** when touching okay and **Not OK** when touching is not okay.
Remember that touch is only okay when the person being touched feels okay about it.

_____

_____

_____

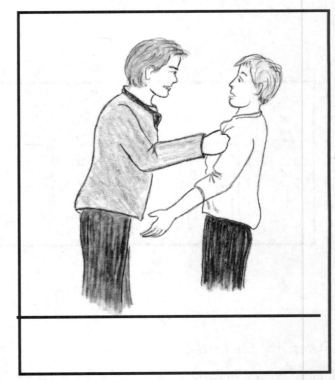
_____

name_____

Read the Body Language

Look at each picture and check all the sentences that are likely true.

_____ The man and woman know each other and are talking about something private.

_____ The woman doesn't want the man to be so close.

_____ They both want to be close.

_____ The man and woman are mad at each other.

_____ They just met.

_____ They know each other and like each other.

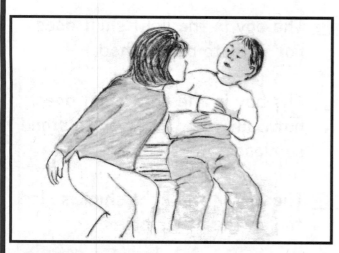

_____ The boy does not like the girl to be so close.

_____ The girl does not want the boy to be so close.

_____ The boy wants the girl to go away.

name_____

Read the Body Language - Part 2

Look at each picture and check all the sentences that are likely true.

_____ They really like each other.

_____ The boy in the light shirt does not want to be touched.

_____ The boy in the dark shirt wants to be close to the other boy.

_____ They really like each other.

_____ The girl likes having the man's arm around her.

_____ The man wants the girl to go away.

_____ The boy in the light shirt does not want to be touched.

_____ The boy in the light shirt does not want the other boy to stand so close.

_____ The boy in the light shirt is glad to see the other boy.

Unit Quiz – Personal Space and Touching

Directions: Check all the answers that are true.

1. A personal space bubble is...
    a. The area around your desk.
    b. An area around you that you want most people to stay out of.
    c. Your room at home.

2. When talking to most people, how far away should you stand?
    a. The length of a ruler.
    b. About 10 feet.
    c. About the length of your arm.

3. What can happen if you get too close to someone?
    a. The person might think you are being a bully.
    b. The person might think you are being too friendly.
    c. The person might not want to be around you because you make him feel uncomfortable.

4. When is it OK for you to go into someone's personal space bubble?
    a. To talk about something private.
    b. When you meet someone for the first time.
    c. To hug your grandmother.

5. When is it OK for someone to come into your personal space bubble?
    a. A stranger comes up to you on the street.
    b. The dentist checking your teeth.
    c. On a crowded bus.

(continued)

6. You go into the doctor's office and there is one stranger sitting in a chair and four empty chairs. Where would you sit?
   a. In the chair next to the stranger.
   b. In a chair that is not right next to the stranger.

7. What do most people do on a crowded elevator?
   a. Look down or stare off.
   b. Say "hi" to everyone on the elevator.
   c. Stand as close to the door as possible.
   d. Stand where there is the most room.

8. How should you touch people to get their attention?
   a. Tap them on the shoulder.
   b. Pat them on the head.
   c. Pull on their clothes.

9. Which of the following are **NOT** OK, except in special situations.
   a. A pat on the back.
   b. Hitting
   c. Touching private parts of the body.
   d. Pushing.

10. What should you do if someone touches you in a way that's not OK.
    a. Say "Stop it!"
    b. Ignore it.
    c. Hit the person.
    d. Tell an adult.

Appendix

Chapter 6 Activity Pages

- 6-1 Saying Hello
- 6-2 Saying Good-bye
- 6-3 Gestures—Greetings
- 6-4 Gestures—Greetings (page 2)
- 6-5 Gestures—Greetings (blank)
- 6-6 Eyebrow Flash Flipbook
- 6-7 Waving—What Does It Mean?
- 6-8 What Does It Mean? (page 2)
- 6-9 Hugging—What Does It Mean?
- 6-10 Hugging Quiz
- 6-11 How to Shake Hands
- 6-12 Handshake Quiz
- 6-13 Bump or No Bump?
- 6-14 Which Greeting?
- 6-15 Draw the Picture #1
- 6-16 Draw the Picture #2
- 6-17 Gestures—Approval
- 6-18 Gestures—Disapproval
- 6-19 Gestures—Approval (blank)
- 6-20 Gestures—Disapproval (blank)
- 6-21 What Does It Mean? #1
- 6-22 What Does It Mean? #2
- 6-23 What Does It Mean? #3
- 6-24 Gestures—Information
- 6-25 Gestures—Information (blank)
- 6-26 What Does It Mean?
- 6-27 What Is the Listener Telling You?
- 6-28 Gesture Bingo Boards
- 6-29 Gesture Bingo Cards
- 6-30 Blank Bingo Board

Saying Hello

When to say hello

- When you see someone you know for the 1st time each day
- To start a conversation
- When you pass someone you know when walking somewhere

How to say hello

- Look at the person
- Smile
- Say hello

Different ways to say hello

Adults	Kids	Strangers

Saying Good-bye

When to say good-bye
- When someone is leaving at the end of the day
- When you are leaving at the end of the day
- When you or someone else is going away for a while
- To end a conversation

How to say good-bye
- Look at the person
- Smile
- Say good-bye

Different ways to say good-bye

Adults	Kids	Strangers

Gestures ~ Greetings

Type	Who uses it	When & where	What it means
eyebrow flash			
wave			
hug			

Gestures ~ Greetings

Type	Who uses it	When & where	What it means
handshake			
fist bump			

Gestures ~ Greetings

Type	Who uses it	When & where	What it means

Eyebrow Flash Flipbook

1. Color pictures in boxes at bottom of the page.
2. Cut out picture boxes along dotted lines.
3. Staple or tape the 2 pictures together.

4. Use a pencil to curl the top page.
5. Roll the pencil back and forth quickly to make the man move.

Waving - What Does It Mean?

Draw a line from the picture to what the person is thinking.

I need help!

Hi! I'm glad to see you.

Good-bye. I'm really sad to see you go.

What Does It Mean?

Draw a line to what the person is thinking

"Hi!"

"I know the answer."

"I need help!"

"Hi!"

Hugging - What Does It Mean?

Draw a line from the picture to what the person is thinking.

This is so sad. I really care about you.

It's so good to see you.

Don't worry. Everything will be OK.

Hugging Quiz

Put a check by all the correct answers. There may be more than one.

1. It is OK to hug:
   a. People in your family.
   b. People you don't know.
   c. Good friends.

2. Sometimes people hug when:
   a. They see a friend they haven't seen for awhile.
   b. They see a stranger at the store.
   c. They are saying good-bye to a good friend.

3. You should **not** hug:
   a. Someone you don't know.
   b. Someone who does not like to be hugged.
   c. Your parents.

4. If you try to hug someone who does not like to be hugged, he will usually:
   a. Smile.
   b. Pull away from you.
   c. Cry.

5. What is a "sideways hug?"
   a. When two people stand facing each other and hug.
   b. When three people hug each other.
   c. When two people stand side to side and hug.

6. When you hug someone who is really sad, it's a way of saying:
   a. "I'm sorry you are sad. I care about you."
   b. "Hello. It's good to see you."
   c. "I've got to go now. See you later."

7. When you hug a friend you haven't seen in awhile, it's a way of saying:
   a. "I'm so sad."
   b. "You are my best friend."
   c. "Hi! It's good to see you."

8. When someone just told you some good news and you hug, it's a way of saying:
   a. "That's great! I'm so happy for you."
   b. "I'm going now. Good-bye."
   c. "It's nice to meet you."

How to Shake Hands

When to shake hands
When someone puts out his or her hand to you.

What to do

1. Look at person and smile.

2. Put your right hand out, thumb up with fingers together.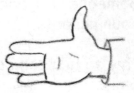

3. Hold other's hand firmly.

 *Not too tight*  *Not too loose*

4. Up and down 3 times.

   ## 1-2-3

Handshake Quiz

Put a check by all the correct answers. (There may be more than one.)

1. If you are not sure whether to shake someone's hand, the best thing to do is to:
    a. Put out your hand.
    b. Wait and see if the other puts out his hand.
    c. Wave at the person.

2. When you shake someone's hand, it's important to:
    a. Look at the person.
    b. Look at your hands.
    c. Smile.

3. Unless there is a reason why you can't, you shake hands with:
    a. Your left hand.
    b. Both hands.
    c. Your right hand.

4. When you put out your hand:
    a. Your thumb should be up.
    b. Your fingers should be together.
    c. Your fingers should be apart.

5. When you shake hands, you should hold the other person's hand:
    a. And squeeze it.
    b. Hold it loosely.
    c. Hold it firmly.

6. When you shake hands, move your hand:
    a. Up and down at least 5 or 6 times.
    b. Up and down 3 times.
    c. Sideways 3 times.

7. People may shake hands:
    a. When they meet someone they don't know.
    b. To congratulate someone.
    c. When they agree on something or make a deal.

8. Which ones are true?
    a. Kids don't shake hands with each other very often.
    b. Adults usually shake hands when they meet someone new.
    c. People always shake hands when they congratulate someone.

Bump or No Bump?

Write <u>Yes</u> if it would be OK for you to give a fist bump in the following situations. If not, write <u>No.</u>

_____ 1. You see your friend in the hall.

_____ 2. You see the principal in the hall.

_____ 3. Another kid comes up to you and says, "I'm mad at you!"

_____ 4. You and a friend are watching a game. Your team scored!

_____ 5. You wish your friend good luck.

_____ 6. You thank the clerk in a store for helping you.

_____ 7. You say hello to the doctor at her office.

_____ 8. Your friend said something really funny.

_____ 9. Your mother is feeling really sad.

_____ 10. A new student just introduces herself to you.

Which Greeting?

Put a check by the best greeting for the situation.

1. Two men are introduced at a business meeting.
   - a. Shake hands
   - b. Fist bump
   - c. Wave

2. Your friend just won a prize.
   - a. Wave
   - b. Eyebrow flash
   - c. Fist bump

3. You are trying to get the attention of someone who is on the other side of the gym.
   - a. Eyebrow flash
   - b. Wave
   - c. Hug

4. Your grandmother came to visit. You haven't seen her for a long time.
   - a. Hug
   - b. Shake hands
   - c. Fist bump

5. You see a friend while you are walking in the hall.
   - a. Hug
   - b. Shake hands
   - c. Wave

6. Someone tells you his name and holds out his hand.
   - a. Shake hands
   - b. Eyebrow flash and smile
   - c. Wave

7. One adult agrees to sell his car to the other.
   - a. Hug
   - b. Eyebrow flash
   - c. Shake hands

8. Someone says, "Let's shake on it."
   - a. Hug
   - b. Fist bump
   - c. Shake hands

Draw the Picture #1

Draw a picture below showing two people greeting each other.

Two friends see each other from a long way off.

Someone is congratulating a friend for winning a contest.

Draw the Picture #2

Draw a picture below showing two people greeting each other.

Two adults are introduced to each other.

A grandmother comes to see her granddaughter, whom she hasn't seen in a long time.

Gestures ~ Approval

Type	When & where	What it means
Head nod		
Thumbs-up		
OK		

Gestures ~ Approval

Type	When & where	What it means
High 5		
Clap		
Cheer		

Gestures ~ Disapproval

Type	When & where	What it means
Head shake		
Thumbs-down		
Finger shake		

Gestures ~ Disapproval

Type	When & where	What it means
Fist		
Nose Wrinkle		
Eye roll		

Gestures ~ Approval

Type	When & where	What it means

Gestures ~ Disapproval

Type	When & where	What it means

What does it mean?

Draw a line to what the person is thinking

"Don't do that!"

Yuck! "I don't like that."

"Yeah! I like that."

"I feel like hitting you!"

"OK."

What does it mean?

Draw a line to what the person is thinking

"Good job!"

"What a stupid idea!"

"I don't like it."

"Yeah! We won!"

"Good luck!"

What Does It Mean? #3

Draw a line to what the person is thinking

"That's a bad idea."

"Yeah! Way to go!"

"I like that idea."

"No! I don't want to do that."

"Yeah! We did it!"

Gestures ~ Information

Type	When & where	What it means
Come here		
Stop		
Shhh		

Gestures ~ Information

Type	When & where	What it means
Can't hear you		
Pointing		
Shrug		

Gestures ~ Information

Type	When & where	What it means
Counting		
Yawn		
Wink		

Gestures ~ Information

Type	Who uses it	When & where	What it means

What Does It Mean?

Draw a line to what the gesture means.

"This is really boring."

"I don't know."

"Be quiet please."

"Come here."

"Stop!"

What Is the Listener Telling You?

Draw a line to what the person is thinking.

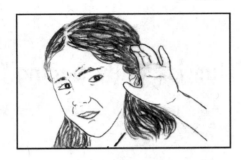

"I hate that noise!"

"Please be quiet."

"Please talk louder."

"I'm listening to what you are saying."

"I'm thinking about something else."

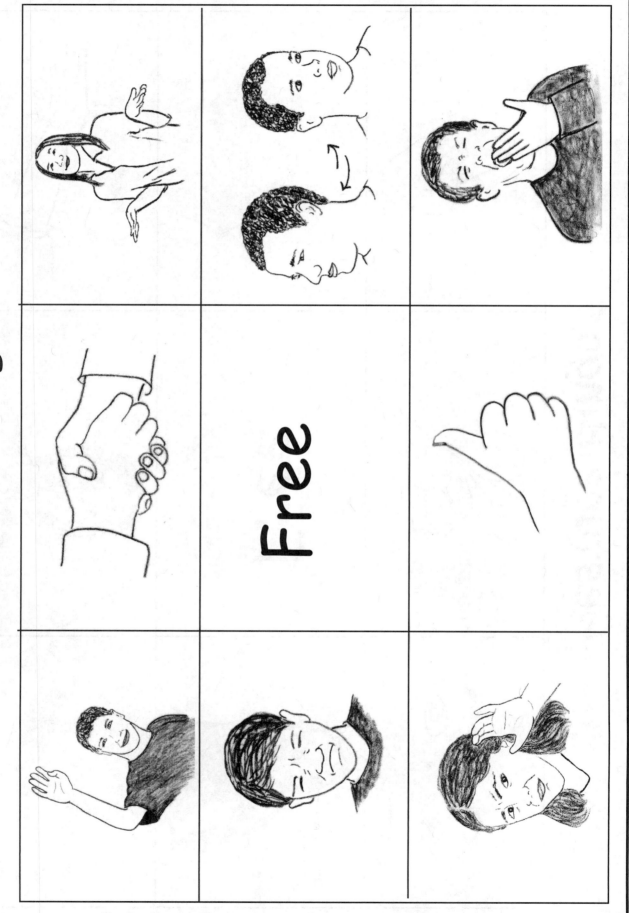

Gesture Bingo

Free

Gesture Bingo

Free

Gesture Bingo

Free

Gesture Bingo

Free

Gesture Bingo

Free

Gesture Bingo Cards

It's nice to meet you.	No. I don't like that.	Yes. I like that.	Hi. I see you.
Good-bye.	I'm tired.	I can't hear you.	I don't know.
Yeah! We did it!	Good job!	I want to say something.	You shouldn't do that!
Too loud.	Stop.	It's so sad.	Go that way.
I want 3 of those.	I need help!	Come here.	I'm really mad at you!
	Oh, brother! That's stupid!	It's so good to see you again.	I'm just kidding.

Gesture Bingo

	Free	

Appendix

Chapter 7 Activity Pages

Understanding Context

Read the following scenarios and circle the word that best describes what the person is feeling.

1. Miguel got up very early this morning and now it's late at night. You are telling him about your trip but he keeps yawning. Miguel is probably...
   a. bored.
   b. tired.

2. You were telling Brittany her hair looks ugly. Now you are telling her about a movie, but she isn't looking at you and isn't saying anything. Brittany is probably...
   a. upset about what you said about her hair.
   b. thinking about what you're saying.

3. Bradley is telling you and Luis a secret. Luis puts his finger to his lips and looks at a teacher who is walking by. Luis is probably ...
   a. trying to tell Bradley that he doesn't want to hear the secret.
   b. afraid the teacher will hear the secret.

4. Halley has been telling Casey about her stamp collection for 10 minutes. Casey keeps looking at the door. Casey is probably...
   a. bored and wants to leave.
   b. thinking about Halley's stamp collection.

5. Evan asked Hunter how to do a math problem. Hunter is frowning and looking away. Hunter is probably...
   a. mad at Evan.
   b. thinking about the math problem.

6. Veronica just told Sophia that she is not coming to her party. Sophia is frowning and looking away. Sophia is probably...
   a. upset because Veronica is not coming to her party.
   b. thinking about things she needs to do.

7. Molly doesn't have her coat and it's cold outside. She is standing, all stiff with her arms crossed while she waits for the bus. Molly is probably feeling...
   a. cold.
   b. mad at the other kids at the bus stop.

8. Trevor is also waiting for the bus in his warm winter coat. He has his arms crossed and is frowning as he stares at Tim. Trevor is probably...
   a. cold.
   b. mad at Tim.

What Are You Thinking?

I want a turn. Pick me!	She keeps talking and talking. I'm so bored.	I'm trying to be very quiet.
I like what you said!	You're just making that up. I don't believe you.	I don't understand. What do you want?
		Yeah! I won 1st prize!
I'm looking for my friend, but I don't see him.	You are wrong!	You surprised me! I didn't hear you come in.
		I don't feel good. My stomach hurts.
I'm really mad at you!	My dog died. I miss her so much!	I don't know the answer. I hope the teacher doesn't call on me.
		There's a bug in my juice. Yuck!

What Are You Thinking?

Index

About the Author

   Pat Crissey has worked in the field of special education for over 20 years, as a special education teacher and autism consultant. She is the author of numerous teaching materials and curricula for children with special needs. Pat received a Bachelor of Science degree in special and elementary education from Illinois State University and completed graduate work in special education at Western Oregon University. She lives in McMinnville, Oregon with her husband and has three grown children and five grandchildren.

153.69071 CRISSEY
Crissey, Pat
Body talk : teaching
   students with
   disabilities about body
   language

R0120261821   ROSWEL

AUG 0 7 2013

ROSWELL
Atlanta-Fulton Public Library